Mother in Heaven

A Gospel Topics Essay Study Guide

CURATED BY
Ashli Carnicelli | Trina Caudle | McArthur Krishna

Mother in Heaven : A Gospel Topics Essay Study Guide

Copyright April 2025 by Ashli Carnicelli, Trina Caudle, and McArthur Krishna, editors.

All rights reserved. Printed in the United States of America. No part of this book may be used or reproduced in any manner without written permission except in the case of brief quotations embodied in critical articles or reviews.

D Street Press, Portland, Oregon, 97239

Cover by Kate Purcell and Jaida Hancock
Design by Andrew Heiss
Layout by Annu Kashyap and Jaida Hancock

Dstreetpress.com

ISBN - 978-1-7342287-2-4

DEDICATION

This book is the culmination of a journey spanning four years, three strangers who are now dear friends, and countless hours with Google Docs and chocolate to create three books honoring and celebrating our Mother in Heaven.

We are changed.

We each arrived at the doctrine of Heavenly Mother's existence at different times and from different angles, but we have been led to the same conclusion:

We know She lives. We know She loves all of Her children. We know She is a full partner to our Father in Heaven and works with Him and our brother Jesus Christ to bring to pass the immortality and eternal life of all humankind.

This book is dedicated to all seekers of the
Divine Feminine, of our Mother.

~ Ashli, Trina, and McArthur

TABLE OF CONTENTS

INTRODUCTION :
THE BEATING HEART OF THE ETERNAL GOSPEL

1. THE NATURE OF GOD — 08
- Malinda Wagstaff Metro — 10
- Rose Datoc Dall — 18

2. BELOVED SPIRIT CHILDREN — 21
- Tom Christofferson — 23
- J. Kirk Richards — 28
- Kimberly Teitter — 29

3. CHERISHED AND DISTINCTIVE DOCTRINE — 36
- Melissa Tshikamba — 38
- Jenna Carson — 39

4. A MOTHER THERE — 43
- Alyssa Wilkinson — 45
- Melissa de Leon Mason — 46
- Martin Pulido — 47

5. SIDE BY SIDE — 63
- Roger and Anne Pimentel — 65
- J. Kirk Richards — 69
- Amy Watkins Jensen — 70

6. DIVINE NATURE AND DESTINY — 76
- Julie Ann Lake-Díaz — 78
- Trina Caudle — 79

7. DESIGNERS OF THE DIVINE PLAN — 86
- Amber Eldredge — 88
- Ashli Carnicelli — 90

8. INFLUENCES FROM BEYOND — 95
- Katie Garner — 97
- Jody Moore — 98

9. CONNECTION — 105
- Sarah Sabey — 107
- Emily Carruth Fuller — 109
- Thomas McConkie — 110

10. ETERNAL PROTOTYPE — 115
- Carly White — 117
- McArthur Krishna — 118
- Michael Workman — 123

11. SACRED KNOWLEDGE — 128
- Lucy Mason — 131
- Patrick Q. Mason — 132

12. HIGHEST ASPIRATION — 138
- Bethany Brady Spalding and Andy Brady Spalding — 140
- Ginger Dall Egbert — 144
- Aubrey Chaves — 145

GLORIOUS — 153
- Jennifer Alvi — 154
- Ashley Workman — 155

Study Helps for each chapter by
Janice McArthur and Carol Pettit

INTRODUCTION

THE BEATING HEART OF THE ETERNAL GOSPEL

Hallelujah! We have a Mother!

In 1909, the First Presidency proclaimed, "All men and women are in the similitude of the universal Father and Mother and are literally the sons and daughters of Deity."

This doctrine anchors our souls to the ongoing restoration of the gospel. Knowing who we are and the purpose of our lives is vital to our eternal progression. Elder Dallin H. Oaks explained, "Our theology begins with Heavenly Parents. Our highest aspiration is to be like Them."

Our Savior Jesus Christ came to the earth to be the bridge. He embodies the attributes of love, kindness, and compassion of both of our Heavenly Parents. His mission and role in the plan of salvation is to assist us in returning to Them, to become like Them— both of our Heavenly Parents.

President Russell M. Nelson teaches the divine harmony of our Heavenly Family working together: "My dear brothers and sisters, Jesus Christ invites us to take the covenant path back home to our Heavenly Parents and be with those we love. He invites us to come, follow me."

> Following the Savior ties us to "the beating heart of the eternal gospel—the love of Heavenly Parents, the atoning gift of a divine Son, the comforting guidance of the Holy Ghost ..." – Elder Jeffrey R. Holland

The Church of Jesus Christ of Latter-day Saints reaffirmed the bold declaration of a Mother in Heaven through the Gospel Topics essay published in October 2015. Elder Dale G. Renlund definitively stated in the April 2022 general conference that this essay is our doctrine. The Gospel Topics essay, located in the online Gospel Library, is six short but mighty paragraphs containing a revolution of doctrinal principles and values. With nineteen references, the doctrine is supported by scriptures, historical research, and modern general conference addresses.

This study guide presents a compilation to dig into the resources provided in the Gospel Topics essay itself and reflections on this cherished doctrine. An investment of time and study can bring our hearts into greater alignment with the heart of the restored gospel of our Heavenly Family. As we seek, our Heavenly Parents promise that we will be uplifted.

INTRODUCTION

"I have Divine Parents and that means that I belong to their household of God. I have rights and privileges and blessings that are associated with being Their child. ... They are teaching me and I can seek and They promise that I will find. I can ask and They promise, 'You will receive.' I am a daughter and I am hungry for knowledge and wisdom and information and progression." — Sister Sharon Eubank

> Blessed are they which do hunger and thirst after righteousness: for they shall be filled. — Matthew 5:6

First Presidency, "The Origin and Destiny of Man," Improvement Era 12 (November 1909): 78. First Presidency: Joseph F. Smith, John R. Winder, Anthon H. Lund.
Dallin H. Oaks, "Apostasy and Restoration," April 1995 general conference.
Russell M. Nelson, "Come Follow Me," April 2019 general conference.
Jeffrey R. Holland, "The Message, the Meaning, and the Multitude," October 2019 general conference.
Dale G. Renlund, "Your Divine Nature and Eternal Destiny," April 2022 general conference.
Sharon Eubank, Relief Society general presidency counselor, 2017-22, "This is A Woman's Church," FAIR Conference, Provo UT, August 8, 2014.

1. THE NATURE OF GOD

"This understanding is rooted in scriptural and prophetic teachings about **the nature of God,** our relationship to Deity, and the godly potential of men and women."

Mother in Heaven essay, paragraph 1

A CORRECT UNDERSTANDING

If men do not comprehend the character of God, they do not comprehend themselves. – Joseph Smith

As we learn of God, we learn of ourselves.

The scriptures and teachings of modern prophets are unequivocal that all humankind is the offspring of God with the potential to return to the heavenly realms through the Atonement of Jesus Christ.

Beginning in Genesis 1, humans were created in the image of God. Psalms 82:6 says explicitly, "Ye are gods; and all of you are children of the most High." Latter-day Saints take this scripture literally — and celebrate!

We learn of the character of God through the Savior's teachings in the Sermon on the Mount (Matthew 5 and 6), with the admonition that we should do likewise — to be merciful, humble, pure in heart, peacemakers. In the New Testament, Peter also outlines attributes of godliness: faith, virtue, knowledge, temperance, patience, kindness, and charity, "for if these things be in you, and abound, they make you that ye shall neither be barren nor unfruitful in the knowledge of our Lord Jesus Christ." (2 Peter 1:3-8)

Primary children have sung for years, "I'm trying to be like Jesus, I'm following in His ways." As we become more like Christ, we develop the character of God and can thus comprehend ourselves more and more.

> Have you ever been told you are just like your mother, or you have your father's smile, or all of your family have the same color eyes? The physical characteristics that we inherit from our parents are obvious. The spiritual characteristics we inherit from our Heavenly Parents have to be developed.
> – President Elaine L. Jack

The Gospel Topics essay, "Mother in Heaven," reiterates the teachings of our divine heritage of both a Father and Mother in Heaven and our potential to become like Them. Let's seek further light and knowledge!

Teachings of the Prophet Joseph Smith, edited by Joseph Fielding Smith, (Salt Lake City: Deseret Book, reprinted 1989) p. 343.
Andrew C. Skinner, Executive Director of the Neal A. Maxwell Institute of Brigham Young University, "The Nature and Character of God," BYU Devotional, April 11, 2006.
Elaine L. Jack, Relief Society general president 1990-97; Young Women general presidency counselor, 1987-90, "Identity of a Young Woman," October 1989 general conference.

THE GOD WHO LOVES ME
Malinda Wagstaff Metro

Joseph Smith once said, "If [people] do not understand the nature of God, they do not understand themselves." He was absolutely correct, but I did not realize the ramifications of this until the last few years.

Tosca

Because I am an opera singer, I'm going to set the scene with a story from my all-time favorite opera: Tosca by Giacomo Puccini. In this show, Tosca is a beautiful, fiery opera singer and a rather pious woman. In Act 2 of the drama, she finds herself faced with an impossible situation. She can either let her love, Mario, be tortured and likely killed, or she can give herself to a corrupt, vile, lustful villain.

The orchestra hums, mimicking both her pounding heart and the pulse of drums taking her love away to the gallows.

She then sings what is (in my opinion) the most beautiful aria ever written.

> I lived for art,
> I lived for love.
> I never hurt anyone in my whole life.
> I secretly went around relieving people of their misfortunes.
> Always, with a sincere faith,
> I said my prayers at the holy tabernacles.
> Always, with a sincere faith,
> I gave flowers to the altar.
> In this hour of pain,
> Why, Lord, why?
> Why do you repay me like this?
> I gave jewels for the Madonna's mantle.
> I gave my songs to the stars and to heaven,
> Which smiled more beautifully because of them.
> In this hour of suffering,
> Why, Lord?
> Why do you reward me like this?

She pays her tithes, worships, says her prayers, enhances her talents, and she expects God to repay her accordingly. Then, when others use their agency to tear apart her safety and take advantage of her vulnerability, she does not know if God is still there. This can happen to anyone. It has happened to me.

THE NATURE OF GOD

The first time I sang that aria "Vissi d'arte," I was so excited. All my favorite singers have recorded it. I felt so lucky to be learning it myself ... until I started working on it with my voice teacher. In the middle of the lesson, I burst into tears. My teacher asked what was wrong, I blurted out,

"I'm not good enough to sing this." I didn't mean vocally. I meant, I did not think that my worth as a person was enough to justify singing the most beautiful aria in the world. I didn't want to sully it with my imperfections.

My teacher is very wise and encouraged me to meditate on where that belief came from.

On my way home, something happened. I realized that I expected God to help me more. I was filled with an anger and a betrayal I had never let myself feel before and it boiled down to this: God, I have worked hard for your kingdom. I've made and kept covenants. I've followed every rule any church leader ever said to me, at great personal cost sometimes. I have paid tithing and gone to activities and prayed and turned the other cheek and tried to avoid taking offense. And THIS is how you repay me? I have NO feelings of self-worth?! I can't do what I want to do most?

> **I had to truly build a relationship with God.**

Somewhere along the way of doing everything all the time, I had picked up the belief that God would love me less or help me less if I couldn't do everything God wanted. Experts call this "love withdrawal" and it can commonly lead to feelings of low self-worth, toxic perfectionism, and religious scrupulosity. I believed in a God that would punish me by holding me back if I didn't perfectly repent of every mistake I had ever made, and I knew I couldn't do that. Despite countless talks of the infinite atonement, I figured I was the one person for whom it wouldn't be enough, or at least not enough in this life.

As I realized that my idea of God was wrong and therefore my idea of myself was wrong, I had to untangle things I thought I knew about God. I had to untangle things I thought I knew about myself. Instead of seeing my relationship with God as a list of things to do and things not to do and a list of things I would receive in exchange (including love and self-worth), I had to truly build a relationship with God.

I won't say this like I am finished with that journey. Is anyone truly ever finished with forming any meaningful relationship? Instead, I now consider myself a permanent scholar of the character of God, and as I study this, I learn many things about myself.

THE NATURE OF GOD

Knowing God

I love learning. My first instinct was to seek to know God the same way I sought to learn something like calculus or Romantic German poetry: I read and studied out of the best books.

Doctrine and Covenants 18:10 says, "The worth of souls is great in the sight of God." For a while, that helped and acted as a powerful mantra, but feelings of self-doubt crept in again.

> *He blessed me that my Heavenly Father loves me, then he paused and said, "and your Heavenly Mother too."*

I studied in the New Testament where Jesus fasts in the wilderness for forty days and Satan comes to tempt Him. In one of the trials, Satan tries to make Jesus doubt who He is; Jesus responds that He knows exactly who He is and Satan could never take that away. That sounded pretty good to me! I wished I could do that. I also noted that Satan was trying to take away Jesus's self-worth, not God.

I studied the teachings of Church leaders about the love of God. Though this is not the Young Women theme I recited each week, I read the first line of the current theme over and over:

"I am a beloved daughter of Heavenly Parents, with a divine nature and eternal destiny." I wanted to believe that and really feel it. I knew that understanding this would be key to redefining my relationship with God.

I remembered a blessing my father gave me during a particularly painful period of my life. He blessed me that my Heavenly Father loves me, then he paused and said, "and your Heavenly Mother too." Asking him about it afterward, he said he heard Her voice and knew She had to be included. I felt Her love in that moment and it comforted and strengthened me to persevere.

So in my journey to understand God, I decided I had to understand my Heavenly Mother as well. I studied the Gospel Topics essay, "Mother in Heaven" and every footnote to learn as much as I could. And I learned a lot. I learned:

- I was made in Her image. While I may sometimes look in the mirror with disappointment, I look like a divine, perfect feminine being.

- She and Heavenly Father are united in purpose, working side by side. That means my dreams and ambitions matter just as much as my husband's, father's,

THE NATURE OF GOD

- and brother's, even if I'm not perfect at everything yet.

- Heavenly Mother and Heavenly Father worked together to create a plan for my life. That plan is divine and the plan is to bring to pass my immortality and eternal life, and we are all here to find joy.

- My Heavenly Parents created me and helped organize the creation of this world. To create is to be like Them.

- My Heavenly Mother is a being of infinite worth and power, and I have the potential to be like Her. Everything I do to develop myself matters and is a practice in being God-like.

- President Jean B. Bingham said, "Do you think our Heavenly Parents want us to succeed? Yes! They want us to succeed gloriously. And do you think They will help us? Absolutely!" [1] That sounded different from the God waiting to punish me and withdraw from me with every mistake. In fact, Elder Holland said, "On a particularly difficult day ... what would this world's inhabitants pay to know that Heavenly Parents are reaching across ... streams and mountains and deserts, anxious to hold them close?" [2]

I realized that I needed to see both of my Heavenly Parents in my understanding of God, or I was missing some of the divinity and worth in myself. I began to see myself as a being of inherent worth, value, and love. I was freed from my fears that I was not good enough or worthy enough to deserve God's love. Doors opened for me to truly get to know God, not just to fear Heavenly Father.

Kennen vs Wissen

In other languages, they have different words for "to know." "Kennen and Wissen," "connaitre and savoir," "conoscere and sapere." The difference is often explained in a textbook as, "one is to know a fact and the other is to be familiar with or know a person." One verb is used to say "I know how to type," and another for "I know Cynthia Erivo."

> **I realized that I needed to see both of my Heavenly Parents in my understanding of God, or I was missing some of the divinity and worth in myself.**

I realized that I knew God in only one way. I had largely relied on knowing God as a fact. Of course there had been other experiences, but I was quick to quote scripture and prophets to explain who God was, rather than explaining how I knew God personally in my own essence and being. It was time to know God with a different verb.

THE NATURE OF GOD

In the scriptures, we see some powerful examples of people who knew God, despite what other people may say were facts.

Hagar

When Abraham and Sarah found that God would give them children, they could hardly believe it so they brought in Hagar to help make sure Abraham would have a son. Institute teacher Colleen Terry Scorseby identifies this as "putting mortal limits on an immortal God." [3]

She named God El Roi: The God who sees me.

Of course, God is more miraculous than that and Sarah was soon pregnant. Hagar was now viewed as no longer important and thrown out into the wilderness. She was likely very frightened and expected to suffer and possibly die.

God came to her in the wilderness and lifted up her son. God told Hagar that a nation would be made of her son. The facts up to this point said Hagar was less than a servant and her son would be nothing. God knew her in a different way and Hagar came to know God in that way. She named God El Roi: The God who sees me. (Genesis 16:13)

The Canaanite Woman

Another example of someone who came to know God, despite what the facts say about God, is the Canaanite woman in Matthew 15.

In this story, she comes to Jesus and asks Him to heal her daughter. After initially ignoring her and then saying He's there to help the children of Israel, He responds, "It is not right to take the children's bread and toss it to the dogs." Ouch. She answers, "Yes, Lord, yet even the dogs eat the crumbs that fall from their masters' table."

Jesus then praises her faith and her daughter is immediately healed. He essentially tells this woman, "Hey. You know I'm here for the Israelites. You're a gentile. Am I even your Messiah?" She has the faith to say, "I may not be of the House of Israel, but I can see what You do, and I believe in You, despite what others say." She named God as someone who cared about her personally. She named Christ as her Savior.

THE NATURE OF GOD

This story shows me that Christ is not just a nebulous Savior who vaguely came for everyone: He really is my Savior. For me. Despite what others may see about my worth, Christ believes I'm worth DYING and LIVING for.

My Journey Continues

I wanted to know God like Hagar and the Canaanite woman! I wanted to know God so much that I could give God a name like "The God who loves me." To continue this journey in a new way, I started to look for God everywhere—not like I had before, "Oh that's a pretty flower. Intellectually, I know God made it. Cool." But to really see God in the world around me and to understand what that could teach me about God and myself.

I read that "God is love" and "The Kingdom of God is within you," so if God is love and within me, God must be love and that love must be within everyone. I looked for pieces of God in everyone.

I found God in:

- The crying baby on the airplane who stopped crying just long enough to smile at a stranger.

- The homeless man taking his dog to an emergency pet clinic, using whatever savings he could.

- The elderly couple holding hands on the bus.

- The opera diva teacher who took the time to apologize for leaving my email unanswered, thus acknowledging my worth and her time.

- The person who voted differently from me but still said hi and asked how I was doing.

> I wanted to know God so much that I could give God a name like "The God who loves me." To continue this journey in a new way, I started to look for God everywhere.

- The colleague who got the role I wanted and sounded so good doing it.

- And so many more people and the love they shared.

THE NATURE OF GOD

And God found me in new ways than before. I came to hear God's many voices. I felt the power and love of God in:

- An opera about motherhood and infertility and souls so esoteric that I had to study for a week before watching the show.

- My anger. Not angry outbursts, but anger that told me when things were unjust and unrighteous, prompting me to make changes.

- The cool earth after a rainstorm.

- Purple flowers. And in the quote from The Color Purple, "I think it [upsets] God if you walk by the color purple in a field somewhere and don't notice it. People think pleasing God is all God cares about. But any fool living in the world can see it always trying to please us back."

> *I find God demanding love more than anything else: love of myself, love of my fellow children of God, love of my enemies.*

- God found me in the mud, crying with heartbreak at disappointment. My Heavenly Parents held me and Christ listened as I wept.

I am coming to see that God is both merciful and just, not vindictive and looking to push me away. I now think of God's justice as Adam Miller describes "what is needed" rather than "what is deserved." [4] I have felt God know exactly what I need, even when it isn't what I necessarily deserved. I have felt Christ's comfort when the world gave me things I didn't deserve. When life is just downright cruel and unfair, Christ has given me what I've needed. I know that I matter because of it. I find God demanding love more than anything else: love of myself, love of my fellow children of God, love of my enemies. And as I find that, the wounds of trauma and pain from my past are healed. I am able to see myself as a beloved daughter of Heavenly Parents.

Chieko Okazaki said, "We live in a world that is held together by love- organized by love, maintained by love, and nurtured by love. Ultimately it will be redeemed by love and even now it is in the process of being redeemed by the love and kindness we offer each other." [5] Love is the power to heal, even deep emotional wounds like not knowing your own value.

THE NATURE OF GOD

I don't say that I know a lot of things about God. I'm still learning. But I believe and hope many things. I know God loves me. I believe God hears my prayers. I believe Christ knows exactly how I feel. I believe I am of infinite worth. I'm not just enough; I am everything to my Heavenly Parents and my Savior, and you are too.

SOURCES

1 Jean B. Bingham, Relief Society general president 2017-22. "How Vast is Our Purpose," BYU Women's Conference, Provo UT, May 5, 2017.
2 Jeffrey R. Holland, "Belonging: A View of Membership," Ensign, April 1980.
3 Colleen Terry Scorseby, seminary and institute teacher, "Latter-day Saint Women" podcast produced by The Church of Jesus Christ of Latter-day Saints, September 16, 2023, churchofjesuschrist.org/media/podcast/latter-day-saint-women-2021-0064-colleen-terry-scoresby-dont-put-mortal-limits-on-an-immortal-god
4 Adam Miller, Original Grace (BYU Maxwell Institute, 2022), 35.
5 Chieko Okazaki, Relief Society general presidency counselor, 1990-97, Being Enough (Bookcraft, 2002), 157.

THE NATURE OF GOD

ONE ETERNAL ROUND

Rose Datoc Dall

THE NATURE OF GOD

STUDY HELPS
The Nature of God

"Jesus answered them, Is it not written in your law, I said ye are gods?"
— John 10:34

"Mother in Heaven" Gospel Topics essay footnotes

Footnote 1: Genesis 1:26-27; Psalm 82:6; Romans 8:16-17; Doctrine and Covenants 132:19-20; Moses 3:4-7.

Footnote 2.1: Gospel Topics essay, "Becoming like God," churchofjesuschrist.org/study/manual/gospel-topics-essays.

Study 1

> "God: (n) the Supreme Being, creator and master of all; any being considered as divine." —Webster's Handy College Dictionary (1972, p.204)

> "God: (n) the supreme being. Being worshipped as the supreme creator and ruler of the Universe; a being or object believed to have supernatural attributes and power and to require worship." —The Merriam-Webster Dictionary (2022, p.314)

How does it change your understanding of the nature of God when you recognize that God is not He, but Them (Heavenly Mother and Heavenly Father)?

What additional characteristics do you feel Heavenly Mother has that are the "nature" of God?

Study 2

> Genesis 1:31; John 10:34; Doctrine and Covenants 20:17; Doctrine and Covenants 20:28.

> No matter to what heights God has attained or may attain, He does not stand alone; for side by side with Him, in all Her glory, a glory like unto His, stands a companion, the Mother of His children. For as we have a Father in Heaven, so also we have a Mother there, a glorified, exalted, ennobled Mother. – Elder Melvin J. Ballard

How do the above verses change when you understand that many scriptural references to God might include Heavenly Mother? Our Heavenly Parents are Creators — what does this tell you about their natures? What have you learned about them as you've exercised your own creative powers?

THE NATURE OF GOD

Study 3

> The glorious vision of life hereafter ... is given radiant warmth by the thought that ... [we have] a Mother who possesses the attributes of Godhood. – Elder John A. Widtsoe [2]

What reverential titles would you give to Heavenly Mother? Why did you choose these titles and how do you interpret them?

Elder Widtsoe taught that our Heavenly Mother possesses the attributes of Godhood. Which of Her many attributes have you discovered/experienced in your life and how?

What do you think life would be like in the Celestial Kingdom if there was not a Heavenly Mother?

Study 4

> We were created ... in the image of our Father and our Mother, the image of our God. – Brigham Young [3]

> Perhaps the most important things for us to see clearly are who God is and who we really are – sons and daughters of Heavenly Parents with a divine nature and eternal destiny. – Sister Michelle D. Craig [4]

What does it mean to you that we can only know ourselves if we know the true nature of God, our Heavenly Parents?

After reading the quotes in this section, on what do you base your thoughts of "She is God?"

Suggested Reading

"A Revolution's Birth," Carly White, *Cherish* book 1, p.51
"Finding God," Carlie Webb, *Cherish* book 2, p.20
"She Is God," McArthur Krishna, *Cherish* book 2, p.42

---

1 Melvin J. Ballard, Sermons and Mission Services of Melvin Joseph Ballard, editor Bryant S. Hinckley, (Salt Lake City: Deseret Book, 1949), 205.
2 John A. Widtsoe, "Everlasting Motherhood,"Millennial Star 90, May 10, 1928: 298; and A Rational Theology: As Taught by the Church of Jesus Christ of Latter-day Saints, Salt Lake City: Deseret Book, 1937: 69).
3 Brigham Young, Discourses of Brigham Young, ed. John A. Widtsoe, Salt Lake City: Deseret Book, 1954: 51.
4 Michelle D. Craig, Young Women general presidency counselor, 2018-23, "Eyes To See," October 2020 general conference.

2. BELOVED SPIRIT CHILDREN

"The Church of Jesus Christ of Latter-day Saints teaches that all human beings, male and female, are **beloved spirit children** of Heavenly Parents, a Heavenly Father and a Heavenly Mother."

Mother in Heaven essay, paragraph 1

TRUE IDENTITY

One of the hallmark statements of President Russell M. Nelson's administration has been the repeated admonition to know who we are as children of God:

> Know the truth about who you are. I believe that if the Lord were speaking to you directly tonight, the first thing He would make sure you understand is your true identity. My dear friends, you are literally spirit children of God. You have sung this truth since you learned the words to "I Am a Child of God." But is that eternal truth imprinted upon your heart? Has this truth rescued you when confronted with temptation? I fear that you may have heard this truth so often that it sounds more like a slogan than divine truth. And yet, the way you think about who you really are affects almost every decision you will ever make.

Let the reality of this eternal identity sink into your soul — it is a stunning truth!

Sister Rebecca L. Craven also encouraged Church members to know our identity as children of God:

> I testify that we are sons and daughters of exalted heavenly parents. Knowing our identity fortifies us against our culture of comparing, complaining, and criticizing. As we consistently strive for refinement in our dignity and demeanor as disciples of Jesus Christ, our confidence will "wax strong in the presence of God." And we will be blessed with an abundance of the Spirit, with personal revelation, and with an increased love of God and our neighbors.

Knowing who we are also lets us know who others are. The Gospel Topics essay, "Mother in Heaven," reminds us that all human beings are the children of Heavenly Parents. Every race, ethnicity, nationality, skin color, sexual orientation, gender identity — all are within the true identity as spiritual offspring of Deity. Your identity as a child of God can guide every decision and interaction.

Russell M. Nelson, "Choices for Eternity," Worldwide Devotional for Young Adults, the Church of Jesus Christ of Latter-day Saints, Salt Lake City. May 15, 2022.
Rebecca L. Craven, Young Women general presidency counselor 2018-23, "The Dignity and Demeanor of Discipleship," Brigham Young University devotional, Provo. October 19, 2021.

BELOVED SPIRIT CHILDREN
Tom Christofferson

> You received your first lessons in the world of spirits from your Heavenly Parents. — President Julie B. Beck

Our experience in mortality of being tutored individually, in critical and often quiet moments by the Holy Spirit, provides an idea of what might have been the experience of learning from Heavenly Mother and Father in pre-earth life. Each of us were intelligences co-eternal with Heavenly Mother and Father and in Their presence, we needed to understand and absorb what Jesus would teach as the greatest of commandments: love. Love demonstrated by desires and visible in actions, that clarifies, directs, distills, and leaves us truly free. Love taught and learned through experiences.

> **Each of us were intelligences co-eternal with Heavenly Mother and Father and in Their presence, we needed to understand and absorb what Jesus would teach as the greatest of commandments: love.**

Two very different and enormously impactful women in my life have given me a conception of premortal tutoring by Heavenly Mother.

In my professional career, the most inspirational mentor and friend was an extraordinary person whose first post-collegiate job was the temporary administrative assistant to an executive in a San Francisco investment management business. Progressively over time, she served as the head of client services, head of sales and client management, head of the largest division within the firm, then as co-chair and finally chairman when it had become the largest institutional asset manager in the world.

> **She had the gift of making those around her want to do more, to be better.**

She had the gift of making those around her want to do more, to be better than their own previous expectations of themselves, because that meant an approximation of the esteem each team member felt from her. There was a lightness in her way of leading, yet clarity and firmness about what needed to be achieved. She was eager to learn, genuinely interested in the perspectives, experiences, and insights of everyone around her, at all levels in the organization and in society.

A great believer in second, third, fourth chances for anyone genuinely trying to do what was asked, while being allergic to posturing and politicking.

> **Perhaps the most important thing I learned in our association was her genuine belief in the goodness of every individual.**

I well remember a time when I was presenting with her to a prospective client in Australia and realized that I had neglected to obtain key data that had been requested when the meeting was arranged several weeks earlier. The flaw was not fatal; we eventually won the business. But the most searing thing was her private comment to me that my omission made it appear that the investment team was less adept and able than was truly the case. Her focus was not that an important win had been put in jeopardy, rather that the work of my colleagues deserved better representation than I had delivered. Revenue, while necessary, was less important than demonstrating respect for the talents and contributions of others.

I had been hired into the firm as its first openly gay executive. As the first woman to hold senior executive positions, she was intrigued by the ways I had learned to show up openly in my career. She invited me to her home often, where I came to know her equally accomplished husband and delighted in their evident enjoyment in each other and pride at the other's accomplishments.

Perhaps the most important thing I learned in our association was her genuine belief in the goodness of every individual. It wasn't surface sentimentality — this was a way of being that she displayed almost unconsciously. She learned that I had identified volunteer opportunities for employees at the corporation I had just left, and lobbied to create a non-profit organization funded by both this firm and its executives personally to benefit the community where the headquarters was located. She asked me to lead it on a voluntary basis. Her instruction to me was that projects supported should be undertaken by employees burning with ideas of how to make a difference, not simply to write checks for good causes. She was the first person I heard use the phrase, "doing well by doing good." She sensed that when enjoying financial success, it is easy to be insulated from the day-to-day challenges of those in the community around us. The most important function of the firm's philanthropy was to connect employees more directly in lifting those who had not had the same opportunity and luck.

More than compassion, she evidenced true empathy for all she encountered. When she married, she became a stepmother to four children, the youngest of whom was only a few years old. Her husband's first wife had mental and emotional challenges, which meant that throughout their marriage, they provided ongoing financial and other forms of assistance to her, as well as ensuring that the children had as much positive interaction with their mother as possible. She spoke of the children's mother as someone with significant challenges who, often heroically, was trying to make the best of her situation.

She quietly battled several different forms of cancer, and at one point she was given a prognosis of about six months to live. True to her character, she and her husband searched for the leading researchers in the emerging field of genetic adaptive cell transfer as a cancer immunotherapy. They funded substantial new research and trials without any expectation that results would arrive in time to benefit her case, but in the hope that others with similar cancers in the future might be saved.

I hope it is obvious why I would tell her story in a book about Heavenly Mother, and in a chapter about each of us as beloved spirit children of Heavenly Parents. While my study of Christ and Heavenly Father begins with searching the scriptures, my effort to comprehend the character and attributes of the Feminine Divine is rooted in the world around me.

The other important woman of great impact in my life is my mother. Some of what I understand of equal partnership has come from observing the interdependent relationship of my parents. My mom worked in our home and exercised her influence not only in the lives of her sons and husband, but by actively identifying other women whom she could assist, mentor, and encourage.

> While my study of Christ and Heavenly Father begins with searching the scriptures, my effort to comprehend the character and attributes of the Feminine Divine is rooted in the world around me.

She made it a practice to particularly notice those who were frequently unseen. A few months after I was born, she was diagnosed with advanced throat cancer. The prognosis was poor, and following extensive surgery it was touch-and-go whether she would survive. Her recovery process was lengthy and painful. With five young sons, ranging in age from twelve years to six months, she needed help beyond what her family could offer. The Relief Society president mentioned a young single mother looking for work. In so many ways, this woman was the opposite of my mother: her husband had abandoned her and her young daughter literally on the side of a road, she had little education, she had a physical handicap that made it very difficult for her to engage socially. But my mother found the ways they were alike: they loved their children, their hearts and minds were receptive and teachable, they knew the living reality of Christ. A lifetime bond of sisterhood was created as each met the needs of the other. Not only were surface appearances unimportant, those surfaces changed as well. This good woman was given opportunity and specific assistance, and later earned a college degree, had a meaningful career that impacted many lives, and raised a wonderful daughter who herself flourished in life.

My mother also demonstrated that love could be returned for hate, kindness for ugliness, beauty for ashes. A single father with several young sons moved across the street from us. Trying to simultaneously provide for and raise his family proved a significant challenge for this dad. To put it charitably, the sons were unruly. They took some delight in lobbing four-letter words and raising the middle digit at passersby, including my mother. One day when they knocked on our door to borrow sugar, I told them because they had been unkind to my mother, I wouldn't give them any. I later reported this to her and expected praise, but she conveyed acute disappointment: "I would never want to refuse food to anyone, and maybe through this we could have become friends."

> **Love grows as we see opportunities to serve, even love that is already deep and profound.**

I recall that someone asked her what I thought was a truly odd question: which one of your sons is your favorite? I, of course, listened keenly albeit surreptitiously. "Whichever one is sick at that moment, or needs extra help, or seems a little discouraged and needs my reassurance." Love grows as we see opportunities to serve, even love that is already deep and profound. Later in life, she said that her greatest happiness came from seeing the relationship her boys had with each other and hearing them laugh together.

Very occasionally, a rather fierce protective instinct reflected her love. At a family reunion when my nephews and nieces were young, she came around the corner to hear some of the boys joking about their gay uncle. My brother reported this experience to me that the boys were a little shaken, never having had their grandmother curtly express her disappointment with them before.

Vitally important to me, both my mentor and my mother grew in understanding over time about the experiences of LGBTQ+ persons. Each developed a respect for the determination of people in their spheres of influence and awareness to be a source of goodness in the world, to achieve dreams and create fulfilling lives. Each woman was a champion for those whose physical, mental, and emotional capabilities were different from most, purposefully reaching out in friendship and to share burdens. Each had nurtured a gift for seeing those on the margins of life, filled with potential but lacking in opportunities.

My conception of respect for personal agency comes from realizing both of these women were attuned to the unique needs and realities of individuals, the distinctive talents and capabilities that could be nurtured, with constant care for the supremacy of each person in their own lives. Like Nephi, they understood each person is an agent to act, not to be acted upon.

Each developed a determination – surely a divine trait – to see the potential in others without judgment for their current situation. Each created an environment of high expectations with equally high support, a recognition that the process of learning could often be more important than the immediate outcomes.

Like me, you have your own mentors and guides whose way of being in the world demonstrates a well-honed ability to love deeply and broadly. Like me, then, a sense of the lessons we will have learned from engagement with our Heavenly Mother calls to our deep yearning to "be ye therefore perfect."

SOURCES

Julie B. Beck, Young Women general presidency counselor, 2002-07; Relief Society general president, 2007-12, "You Have a Noble Birthright," April 2006 general conference.

BELOVED SPIRIT CHILDREN

WE HAVE SET OUR RAINBOW UPON THE CLOUDS

J. Kirk Richards

HEAVENLY FAMILY, THE HOUSEHOLD OF GOD
Kimberly Teitter

> In the beginning God created the heaven and the earth. And the earth was without form, and void; and darkness was upon the face of the deep. And the Spirit of God moved upon the face of the waters. And God said, Let there be light: and there was light. — Genesis 1:1-3

And as that light moved, dividing darkness from light, and as the splendor of creation bloomed, and the stars appeared, and the earth yielded seed and fruit, and the fishes and the animals were made to multiply — where was our Mother?

Then and now, a belief in Heavenly Mother represents the purest embodiment of faith, a deep rooting in the power of the unseen.

Did She source the breath of life that the Lord God breathed into the nostrils of man? Did She till the dust until the flowers bloomed? Did She model dominion over the fish of the sea, and the fowls of the air, and every creeping thing, with a tender and careful hand? When Eve emerged from the rib, the crowning act of creation, did our Mother fill her spirit with the wisdom to choose? When the blood of Abel spilled on the ground, did our Mother weep while our Father cursed? When Enoch looked over the earth with his heart swelling wide as eternity, was it our Mother who cradled his soul until it had the space to expand?

The doctrine of Heavenly Mother, a "cherished and distinctive belief among Latter-Day Saints," [1] seems to have evolved both as an extension of logic and as a searching hand in the dark for those who sought hope in the light of the Restored gospel. Many early mentions of Heavenly Mother came in the context of death and loss, a mournful yearning for something higher and better in the eternal realm. Then and now, a belief in Heavenly Mother represents the purest embodiment of faith, a deep rooting in the power of the unseen. And what was the substance of hope in Her presence? In 1920, while reflecting on the First Vision, Susa Young Gates remarked:

> That wonderful appearance in the Grove, at Palmyra, held in its heart, like the half-opened calyx of a rose, all the promises of future development for woman ... There was to be no bond and free in Christ Jesus, but all were to be free ... The divine Mother, side by side with the divine Father, the equal sharing of equal rights, privileges, and responsibilities, in heaven and on earth, all this was foreshadowed in that startling announcement of the Son: "They were all wrong! They draw near to me with their lips, but their hearts are far from me!" [2]

Even as the light rested on Joseph and revealed two personages in male form, Susa still saw our Mother there, in the freedom that our divine connection to our denied the power thereof." [3] In contrast, through the promise of the gospel, continuing revelation, and the gift of agency, men and women could choose to together "stumble along ... facing the rising sun of the coming day of peace and power." [4]

How revolutionary it was in her time — or even in ours — to think about men and women working together toward a common goal, occupying the same respect and consideration, being free to learn together, and err together, and come to God together. Conceptualizing our mortal journey as a family shepherded by Heavenly Parents makes us "no more strangers and foreigners, but ... of the household of God." (Ephesians 2:19)

> **What would it be like if our Mother's existence reminded us to look to Her when we feel tempted to look down upon our brother, or harshly judge our sister, or cut off our siblings from our embrace?**

But what have we done with Our Family? Somehow, even with the promise of the family being the eternal unit of the heavens, we have made ourselves into societies where we see our differences, where we sow divisions, where we create narratives about our heavenly family members that makes us justify seeing them as our foes. And sometimes, we do this in the name of preserving our families, in protecting our faith and our practice. We do this and lay our heads to sleep at night praying for peace, while our Parents weep —

> Behold these thy [siblings]; they are the workmanship of [our] own hands, and [we] gave unto them their knowledge, in the day [we] created them ... and unto thy [siblings] have I said, and also given commandment, that they should love one another, and that they should choose [us, their Family]; but behold, they are without affection, and they hate their own blood. — Moses 7:32-33

What would it be like if our Mother's existence reminded us to look to Her when we feel tempted to look down upon our brother, or harshly judge our sister, or cut off our siblings from our embrace? Could we go to Her to help us heal, to seek help in knitting our hearts together in unity? If we had cognizance of our divinely connected heritage through our Mother, perhaps we would be more willing to stumble together instead of trudge through the lone and dreary world with only our own devices. Maybe our ears would be inclined to both justice and mercy, and our hearts attuned to Zion among us. We would intimately hear the call to mourn with those that mourn and to strengthen the feeble knees, because we all would recognize our dependence on the same Parents who have not left us to beg in vain.

BELOVED SPIRIT CHILDREN

What would it be like if our Mother's existence reminded us of the power and potential for good we all possess? When our brother Moses was tempted by Satan (Moses 1:12-22), he recognized that his identity as a son of God gave him the ability to discern his own power, and the capacity to resist power that would have no heavenly gain. What if our Mother was there to remind him, like the mothers of the Stripling Warriors, who he was and whose he was? And when Jesus was tempted by Satan in the wilderness, did our Mother's presence allow Him to resist temptation while modeling for His spirit brother a better way?

Though many people do it every day, I couldn't imagine living without my own earthly mother's influence in my life. I couldn't imagine not being able to source it either, to not be able to recognize the threads of her life that have become woven into mine. It's a luxury that I know isn't afforded to all people to understand myself in part through my inheritance from her. I see the same desire to serve the Lord in a more outward way; the same quirky willingness to try new big things while keeping the small things as routine as possible; the same belief that gaining an education and serving others through my own employment blesses my family, even on days where it feels impossible to manage.

I often wonder if our de facto context of a Heavenly Single Parenthood — one that gives us the image of a loving Father, a sacrificing Brother, and the rest of us siblings being the family fix-it projects — leaves us with a shattered or occluded mirror to gaze into each day, as we try to see the God in us. I remember sitting in class as a youth and hearing an adult leader say that she felt we as women would surely be valuable in creating worlds in the next life: for example, being able to say that this butterfly should be pink instead of blue. I recently read a hot take that without men, the Church would be nothing but a women's community group. As a woman, I wonder how much knowledge our Mother has to bestow upon us about our capacity for creation and rooting in our divine

> **I couldn't imagine not being able to source it either, to not be able to recognize the threads of her life that have become woven into mine.**

potential, even as Her daughters underestimate that divine drive in themselves. I wonder if dutiful men, seeking to pattern their lives of service after the Father or the Son, would permit themselves to embrace the divine Feminine modeled through the tenderness and mercy of our Savior, and be able to care for their stewardships more effectively.

I am reflecting on this subject while being surrounded by my two children, my literal pieces of heaven on earth. My five-year-old lays next to me, her slumbering soul subconsciously filling herself into every would-be empty space between us.

My eleven-year-old sits on my feet, wearing the same winter coat my mother gave to me when I was the same age. As I look at her, my eyes spontaneously fill with tears, my soul inextricably linked to these two beings whose earthly features I had a hand in creating. My own heart beams with the expanse of the eternities; I see the creators they are growing to be while remembering the small fragile beings I once held in my arms, even as I battle flailing sleepy limbs and try to recall from mind the intricacies of middle school crushes.

Many people have only experienced that love in the context of their own families, but there have been precious few times in life where I met people the Lord placed in my path and instantly felt the same soul connection that transcended time and space. They are people whose spirits I would expect to recognize and be drawn in any divine form; they are people whose heavenly potential I invest in with the sameenthusiasm as with my two girls. Recently, one of those people hurt me deeply, in a way that shattered my faith in my own ability to see beyond the relational complications of this world and live celestially. Where I had once felt buoyed by their love and regard, I was left feeling confused and empty, with eternal expanses of pain where there was once enough joy to stretch across humanity.

Like many desperate and heartbroken calls I have placed to my earthly parents over the years, I stumbled out of bed early one morning after countless sleepless nights trying to find healing on my own, and made a trip to my Heavenly Parents' house instead. I swiftly maneuvered into the temple parking lot as fresh snow began to fall, desperately trying to consecrate my urgency to commune with the Divine to make up for a speed beyond earthly limits. I misplaced my temple recommend, which I found safely tucked back in my car, and missed the session I was aiming to attend. The woman at the front desk no doubt saw my forlorn – bordering on angry – face, reached into the depths of our sisterly connection, and reminded me that I could do sealings. I dressed for the occasion and moved upstairs to the sealing room, my clothing echoing the previous weeks' haunting pain of assuming worth I did not deserve.

> **Many people have only experienced that love in the context of their own families, but there have been precious few times in life where I met people the Lord placed in my path and instantly felt the same soul connection that transcended time and space.**

However, as I entered the sealing room, my self-consciousness began to thaw as the sealer welcomed me in, saying, "We could really use you today." My presence there allowed daughters to be eternally bound to their parents, which I had not been able to consider as a pressing needuntil being in the room with their anxious spirits. At one point, I sat across from a man whose hands were clearly weathered and even dirtied by the nature of his earthly work; I watched myself extend my hand to him without flinching, my spirit submerged in the reality of our connection as heavenly siblings.

I felt my Heavenly Mother's presence there, recognizable in the feminine energy woven through the love I have for my own family. I saw the worn hand of my brother across from me and realized that we are all worn, we are all striving to be clean, we are all stretching toward that love our Parents have to offer us. I felt my Mother guiding my heart to forgive the friend who hurt me, to see that person as a traveler on a divine path that sometimes is occluded by our own mortal eyes. From that day, I slowly began to restore my faith in a dual Parentage that is steadily guiding Their children home.

As we usher in the gathering of Israel and await our grand Family reunion, will we recognize our Mother when we see Her? I hope so; but more importantly, I hope that our acts of creation, of nurturing, of shepherding Her children home, will prepare us to see Her for who She is, recognize our image in Hers, and allow Her to welcome us into Her bosom of rest.

> *I felt my Heavenly Mother's presence there, recognizable in the feminine energy woven through the love I have for my own family.*

SOURCES

1 "Mother in Heaven," Gospel Topics essays, churchofjesuschrist.org/study/manual/gospel-topics-essays.
2 Susa Young Gates, Relief Society general board member, 1911-22, "The Vision Beautiful," Improvement Era 23 (April 1920):542.
3 Joseph Smith History 1:19.
4 Gates, "The Vision Beautiful."

STUDY HELPS

Beloved Spirit Children

"Mother in Heaven" Gospel Topics essay footnotes

Footnote 2.2: "Mother in Heaven," Encyclopedia of Mormonism (1992). By Elaine Anderson Cannon.

Footnote 3: "History of the Young Ladies' Mutual Improvement Association of the Church of Jesus Christ of Latter-Day Saints," Deseret News (1911), p. 16. By Susa Young Gates. Summary: Zina Diantha Huntington recalled that when her mother died in 1839, Joseph Smith consoled her by telling her that in heaven she would see her own mother again and become acquainted with her eternal Mother.

Footnote 6: "The Origin of Man," Improvement Era, Nov. 1909, p. 75-81. By the First Presidency (President Joseph F. Smith).

Study 1

> "Spirit: (n) the inspiring principle or dominant influence; Soul; the nature of a person; disposition; the essence or real meaning" —Webster's Handy College Dictionary (1972, p.436)

> "Spirit: (n) a soft, giving force; pious; devout." —The Merriam-Webster Dictionary (2022, p.703)

What do the above definitions tell you about your eternal nature?

Parents revere their children; why and how does this happen? How do you feel our Heavenly Parents are able to revere Their billions of spirit children?

What do the above definitions tell you about the nature of your Heavenly Mother?

Study 2

> A Heavenly Mother interacts with the Trinity in a certain and irresolvable sense. As there can be no spirit children without Her, presumably there would be no Son without Her … It should be no surprise then, that most Mormon leaders could not understand how Father or Mother could be divine alone. For either to be fully God, each must have a partner, with whom to share the power of endless lives. — David Paulsen [1]

As earthly parents each bring different gifts and perspectives to their parenting, so do our Heavenly Parents. How do you envision Their divine partnership that functions perfectly? How might this partnership impact Their parenting?

How can we pattern our partnerships on Them? How do you envision your own eternal partnership?

How does it feel to know you are a spirit child of Heavenly Mother and Father?

Study 3

> The First Presidency, under Joseph F. Smith, issued a statement ... 'man as a spirit, was begotten and born of Heavenly Parents, and reared to maturity in the eternal mansions of the Father,' as an 'offspring of celestial parentage,' and further teaches that 'all men and women are in the similitude of the universal Father and Mother and are literally the sons and daughters of Deity'. — Elaine A. Cannon [2]

> Parenthood requires both father and mother, whether for the creation of spirits in the Premortal life or of a physical tabernacle on earth. A Heavenly Mother shares parenthood with the Heavenly Father. This concept leads Latter-day Saints to believe that She is like Him in glory, perfection, compassion, wisdom, and holiness. — Elaine A. Cannon [3]

What does the word Similitude mean? How does that apply to being beloved spiritual children?

What do you think President Smith meant by spiritual maturity? What does premortal spiritual maturity mean to you?

What experiences have you had when you felt the love of Heavenly Parents?

Suggested Reading

"You Are", Mari Christina Tomkinson Heward, *Cherish* book 2, p.109

1. David L. Paulsen and Martin Pulido, "'A Mother There': A Survey of Historical Teachings About Mother in Heaven," BYU Studies 50: 1 (2011), p.10.
2. Elaine Anderson Cannon, "Mother in Heaven," Encyclopedia of Mormonism (1992).
3. Cannon, ibid.

3. CHERISHED AND DISTINCTIVE DOCTRINE

"The **doctrine** of a Heavenly Mother is a **cherished and distinctive** belief among Latter-day Saints."

Mother in Heaven essay, paragraph 1

CHERISHED AND DISTINCTIVE DOCTRINE

A LIGHT TO THE WORLD

The Gospel Topics essay, "Mother in Heaven," calls the knowledge of Mother in heaven "a cherished and distinctive belief." The scriptures teach that our knowledge of gospel truths should not be hidden under a bushel, but held up as a candle to guide and influence others. "It giveth light unto all that are in the house." (Matthew 5:15-16)

Light is worth celebrating!

> I have heard it said by some that the reason women in the Church struggle to know themselves is because they don't have a divine female role model. But we do. We believe we have a Mother in Heaven. … Furthermore, I believe we know much more about our eternal nature than we think we do; and it is our sacred obligation to express our knowledge, to teach it to our young sisters and daughters, and in so doing to strengthen their faith and help them. — Sister Patricia R. Holland

Sharing spiritual knowledge is encouraged in church classroom settings, public testimony meetings, and even on social media. Our different strengths and ways to spread the light of the gospel are as unique as we are. You may feel inclined to share your love for our Heavenly Mother and Father in a one-on-one intimate conversation. You may bear testimony of Heavenly Parents in sacrament meeting. You may be prompted to broadcast a statement of faith through the megaphone of social media.

However you are inspired to learn and share, please consider this study guide an invitation to follow Sister Holland's counsel and learn of Heavenly Mother.

Everyone has a candle. Let's spread the light!

Patricia Holland, Young Women general presidency counselor, 1984-86, "One Thing Needful: Becoming Women of Greater Faith in Christ," Ensign (October 1987): 26.

QUEEN OF HEAVEN

Melissa Tshikamba

IN HER HAND
Jenna Carson

My brain jolted when I heard Bobby McFerrin sing these lines:

> The Lord is my shepherd. I have all I need.
> She makes me lie down in green meadows.
> Beside the still waters She will lead.

My reaction was visceral. Moved, my eyes began to water. At the same time, I felt uncomfortable. I had only ever interpreted Jesus as the subject of the 23rd Psalm, and the feminine pronouns felt subversive. Yet hearing the language of the Psalm reorganized to reflect the love of a woman touched something deep in me.

I was gathered with a group of interfaith chaplain colleagues, and an Episcopal priest had played the song to open our meeting. When the song ended, the priest — a woman — said, "I'm going to play it again."

I closed my eyes. This time, I exhaled my discomfort and told myself to just listen, just feel.

> Even though I walk through a dark and dreary land,
> There is nothing that can shake me,
> She has said She won't forsake me, I'm in Her hand.

When the song ended, I swallowed, wiped traces of mascara from beneath my eyes, picked up my water bottle, and took a drink. I looked at the faces of my colleagues, blurred from my tears, expecting to find similar evidence of emotion among them. No one else, however, seemed particularly touched. We moved on with our meeting.

> *I had only ever interpreted Jesus as the subject of the 23rd Psalm, and the feminine pronouns felt subversive. Yet hearing the language of the Psalm reorganized to reflect the love of a woman touched something deep in me.*

A few hours later, as our time together came to a close, I asked the group about the song. "I am curious how that hit you," I asked my colleagues, each of them chaplains from different Catholic and Protestant denominations. I pointed out the pronouns and wanted to know what those pronouns meant to each of them theologically.

CHERISHED AND DISTINCTIVE DOCTRINE

"God has no gender, but language matters, so we sometimes use female pronouns for God for purposes of inclusion," explained one chaplain. The others nodded in agreement.

I briefly explained that members of the Church of Jesus Christ of Latter-day Saints believe in a Heavenly Mother, a counterpart to God the Father. This is why the lyrics so deeply touched me. They made Her more real to me; She was not a passive, elusive figure, but a shepherd holding me in Her hand.

The cherished, distinctive doctrine of Heavenly Mother in Latter-day Saint theology suggests that an embodied Mother, along with an embodied Savior and Father, understands embodiment through experience. To me as a woman, this embodiment matters. On a very primal level, it helps me feel understood when I am bleeding and weeping and hurting.

As a female chaplain, women regularly come to me seeking spiritual guidance. As these women share their stories, I often bear witness to the pain and suffering of their bodies. When I think about Mother God, I think about Her holding the bodies of these women: a 19-year-old who attempted to take her life in the middle of a messy divorce. An engaged woman raped by a classmate. A pregnant newlywed planning an abortion, terrified to repeat the mistakes her birth mom made, convinced she wasn't ready for a child. A woman whose husband raped her while she breastfed their daughter. A woman who deployed and, in combat — her body so traumatized from near-constant shelling — stopped bleeding altogether. She returned home without a period and never got it back. "I grieved that," she said. "I had wanted another baby."

> **To me as a woman, this embodiment matters. On a very primal level, it helps me feel understood when I am bleeding and weeping and hurting.**

With these women, I wept and witnessed their weeping. I had not carried all the things that they had, but like them, my body had bled, and like them, my body had been vulnerable. Like some of them, I had grieved losing an unborn child.

Women's bodies bleed with each other, for each other, birth each other. We suffer and succor one another. Our children suckle and grow and know the love and power of mothers. I cannot speak for all women, but I believe I will always long to feel held in my mothers' hands: in the hands of my biological mother, in the hands of other women who love me, and in the hands of an Eternal Mother God.

STUDY HELPS
Cherished and Distinctive Doctrine

"Mother in Heaven" Gospel Topics essay footnotes

Footnote 2.2: "Mother in Heaven," Encyclopedia of Mormonism (1992). By Elaine Anderson Cannon.

Footnote 4: "Come to Me," in "Poetry, for the Times and Seasons," Times and Seasons 6 (Jan. 15, 1845), p. 783. By W.W. Phelps.

Study 1

> "Cherish: (v) to treat with tenderness and affection; to give warmth, ease and comfort to. To hold dear, to embrace with affection, to foster and encourage. To treat in a manner to encourage growth by protection, aid." —Webster's American Dictionary of English Language (1828)

What does *cherish* mean to you? How do you cherish the doctrine of a Heavenly Mother?

Why is it important to cherish the concept of having Heavenly Parents, especially a Heavenly Mother?

Make a list of the verbs from the above definition that are used to describe cherish. What actions have you shown to your Heavenly Parents and other loved ones to demonstrate that you cherish them?

Make a list of things you cherish, then categorize them. For example:

- People: spouse, children
- Objects: a family heirloom, a meaningful gift
- Intangibles: peace, the gospel

Why are these things important to us, even the objects? Why do we cherish them? How do these things relate to the meaning of *cherish*? How do you feel that they relate to Heavenly Mother?

Study 2

> "Distinct: (adj) separateness, different, well defined, not blurred, unmistakable."
> — Webster's Handy College Dictionary (1972)

CHERISHED AND DISTINCTIVE DOCTRINE

> Distinctive: (adj) different, making a difference, characteristic. A feature that helps to distinguish a person or thing; capable of being classified." – Vocabulary.com/dictionary

What does the term distinctive doctrine mean to you? How do you feel the doctrine of Heavenly Mother is distinct?

What are some other distinctive doctrines within The Church of Jesus Christ of Latter-day Saints? What makes them unique? How is your testimony affected by this perspective?

Study 3

> Today the belief in having a Mother in Heaven is implicit in the Latter-Day Saint thought. Though scriptures contain only hints, statements from Presidents of the Church over the years indicate that human beings have a Heavenly Father as well as a Heavenly Mother. – Elaine A. Cannon

What does Sister Cannon's statement mean to us today? To others of different faiths?

What information or concepts do you have to support your answer?

Why do you think the concept of Heavenly Mother is hard for some people to accept? Why have you been able to accept our Heavenly Mother?

If a person of a different faith asked why you believe in Heavenly Mother, what would you tell them to explain your belief?

Suggested Reading

"Cherished is a Verb," Trina Caudle, *Cherish* book 2, p.117
"Cherish," McArthur Krishna, *Cherish* book 1, p.67

Elaine Anderson Cannon, "Mother in Heaven," Encyclopedia of Mormonism (1992).

4. A MOTHER THERE

"In the heav'ns are parents single?
No, the thought makes reason stare.
Truth is reason—truth eternal
Tells me I've **a Mother there**."

Mother in Heaven essay, paragraph 2

HEAVENLY MOTHER MATTERS

The Gospel Topics essay, "Mother in Heaven," testifies, "Just as we have a Father in Heaven, we have a Mother in Heaven."

Multiple prophets, apostles, and women leaders of the Church have stated repeatedly, "Motherhood is more than bearing children, though it is certainly that. It is the essence of who we are as women. It defines our very identity, our divine stature and nature." – Sister Sheri Dew. We as a church culture would never discount the role of an earthly mother and say that she doesn't matter, that she is not essential to her family – let's not discount our Mother in Heaven either!

Elder Holland advocates for this appreciation as well:

> To Mother Eve, to Sarah, Rebekah, and Rachel, to Mary of Nazareth, and to a Mother in Heaven, I say, "Thank you for your crucial role in fulfilling the purposes of eternity." To all mothers in every circumstance, including those who struggle – and all will – I say, "Be peaceful. Believe in God and yourself. You are doing better than you think you are. In fact, you are saviors on Mount Zion, and like the Master you follow, your love 'never faileth.'" I can pay no higher tribute to anyone.

Heavenly Mother matters. She is essential to the human family.

Sheri Dew, Relief Society general presidency counselor, 1997-2002, "Are We Not All Mothers?" October 2001 general conference.
Jeffrey R. Holland, "Behold Thy Mother," October 2015 general conference.

MIDNIGHTS
Alyssa Wilkinson

Every night
Around midnight
I crack open the door to my children's room
And I tiptoe across the floor
(Making sure to avoid the spots that creak)
And I kneel close
Soaking in every detail
Their tousled heads resting on their pillows
The curve of their noses
The satin skin of their cheeks
I kiss their foreheads and whisper

I love you
I love you
I love you

Hoping, somehow, that my words will soak
Into their dreams
And into their bones
And that they will become a part of them
Echoing inside as they go throughout their daily lives

I love you
I love you
I love you

I find myself wondering now
How many deep, dark midnights in my life
Has my Mother done the same
Cracking open the veil
And tiptoeing across Heaven
To gather near to me
Her slumbering child
Taking in every little detail
And smiling to Herself
As She brushes the hair from my brow
(And perhaps a tear from my cheek)

And pulls me close
Whispering

I love you
I love you
I love you

A MOTHER THERE

BOUGAINVILLEA 2024

Melissa de Leon Mason

The vibrant hues of Bougainvillea dotted the landscape of my childhood and any time I visit a place where they grow I'm stuck by a sense of homecoming. For me, they are more than just flowers; they are symbols of belonging and comfort, a kind of home that transcends physical spaces. In creating this quilt, I was inspired by the idea of Heavenly Mother and the subtle yet powerful ways Her presence manifests in the world around us. Just as the bougainvillea thrives in unexpected corners, Her love and influence appear in the quiet details of daily life — offering comfort, strength, and beauty.

"A MOTHER THERE":
Reflections and Amendments After 14 Years

Martin Pulido

After writing on Christian convergences on the divine feminine in his article "Are Christians Mormon?", the late David L. Paulsen received a research grant from the Women's Research Institute at Brigham Young University to examine LDS Christian teachings on Heavenly Mother. The historical research put into this project leveraged archives, university libraries, and digital collections to provide a textured exploration of Heavenly Mother since the earliest years of the restored church. [1] Partnering with research assistants, of which I served as lead, we compiled, annotated, and critically analyzed relevant sources. Subsequent presentations Dr. Paulsen and I gave at different symposia became the basis for a paper, eventually published in 2011 by BYU Studies as "A Mother There: A Survey of Historical Teachings about Mother in Heaven." [2]

> Heavenly Mother wasn't spoken about in LDS circles because She was considered too sacred. While we found that this belief among Latter-day saints emerged in the mid-20th century, this viewpoint did not receive any known endorsement or encouragement from church leaders in any time period.

We structured our paper in the university journal to address a common thread we saw in public discourse and academic writings: namely, the suggestion that Heavenly Mother wasn't spoken about in LDS circles because She was considered too sacred. While we found that this belief among Latter-day saints emerged in the mid-20th century, this viewpoint did not receive any known endorsement or encouragement from church leaders in any time period. We suggested this viewpoint was a purely cultural phenomenon. Holy topics should be spoken of with deep respect, such as our holy temple, our holy God, the holy priesthood, the holiness of Christ. But the sacredness of a subject does not preclude us talking about the topic; rather, it structures our attitude in how we go about discussing it. It fosters reverence, not silence. [3]

As a result, we laid out this perspective and contrasted it with the material gathered from male and female church leaders on Heavenly Mother and Her various roles. She was commonly described as a divine being involved in the creation of the world, the formation of the plan of salvation, the shepherding and care of humanity now, and the destiny of humanity in the hereafter alongside our Heavenly Father. We felt it necessary to emphasize those other roles, due to another theme in discourse that Heavenly Mother was viewed only functionally as an eternal birther. The article also delved into other matters where appropriate, such as questioning and discounting exegesis that suggested God was an androgynous being, and examining the relationship between Heavenly Parents and the trinity.

However, the article still possessed professed gaps. Some of these limitations were methodological. Namely, the poor availability of searching international and non-digitized materials limited the documents we could examine. This gave undue emphasis on English-published materials and a patchy representation of church writings spanning roughly from 1930 to 1970. Even with this in mind, we felt confident that what we'd compiled would not be fundamentally overturned by later research but only fleshed out further. Indeed, the church has since filled in many gaps with the availability of digital records from this time period and from international sources. This originally neglected material has been evaluated and only builds upon what came before. [4] No discovery has been made of a church leader encouraging "sacred silence," and additional research has only shown that Heavenly Mother was a cherished doctrine among Latter-day Saints across the globe. [5]

Outside of methodological constraints, the "A Mother There" article gave emphasis to teachings of LDS Christian church leadership. This limitation of scope ignored broader church literature, lay member gospel reflections, and literary traditions, which are worthy of study. Some of this has been rectified since the publication of a "A Mother There." For instance, *Dove Song: Heavenly Mother in Mormon Poetry*, published in 2018, filled in a lot of the historical literary gaps, including the first instance of Heavenly Mother published in February 1844, albeit to the neglect of historical non-poetic LDS Christian prose that still must find an outlet. [6] An explosion of literary and artistic expression has followed with many new published works, including children's books (kicked off by *Our Heavenly Family, Our Earthly Families*), and a renaissance of Heavenly Mother portrayal in the visual arts, which has trended since 2012. A massive painting of Heavenly Parents by Caitlin Connolly hangs in the Church History Library. All these deserve their proper attention but fell outside the purview of research for "A Mother There."

Teachings of Church Leaders in Subsequent Years (2011 - 2024)

Since the 2010 publication of the BYU Studies article, church leaders have continued to discuss Heavenly Mother and Heavenly Parents. While much of the content reflects earlier teachings[7], there are also new areas of focus. In reviewing statements from the past 14 years, five themes stand out:

1. Our belief in loving, personal Heavenly Parents is fundamental to the LDS Christian worldview.

While President Dallin H. Oaks has repeated that "our theology begins with heavenly parents," this position has been expanded upon by other church leaders. [8] For instance, in October 2019, Elder Jeffrey R. Holland expressed that new converts to the faith can be distracted by many doctrinal and cultural concepts. As a result, existing members "must point past the hustle and bustle and concentrate them [new members] on the meaning of it all, on the beating heart of the eternal gospel — the love of Heavenly Parents, the atoning gift of a divine Son, the comforting guidance of the Holy Ghost, the latter-day restoration of all these truths and so much more." [9] It is telling that Elder Holland mentioned Heavenly Parents' love as the first thing with which to anchor an LDS Christian convert.

Elder Ronald A. Rasband, in a separate October 2016 conference address, cautioned latter-day saints, who may be dealing with struggles of faith, to not forget sacred truths. The one Elder Rasband most hoped members would never forget, was "first and foremost that we are sons and daughters of living and loving Heavenly Parents, who desire only our eternal happiness." [10] On a similar occasion, Elder M. Russell Ballard asked members considering leaving the faith to first ponder, "Where will you go to find others who share your belief in personal, loving Heavenly Parents, who teach us how to return to Their eternal presence?" [11] Asked in this fashion, Elder Ballard emphasized that such a belief is rare and deeply meaningful to the LDS Christian community.

In a different conference address, Elder Ballard framed mortal life as a preparation for eternal exaltation, with Heavenly Parents serving as both the origin and the destination in a grand "family story." He shared, "The purpose of mortal life and the mission of The Church of Jesus Christ of Latter-day Saints is to prepare the sons and daughters of God for their destiny — to become like our Heavenly Parents. The gospel story is a family story — nothing more, nothing less. It begins with Heavenly Parents, and it ends with children making their way through the sometimes exhilarating, sometimes overwhelming challenges of mortality and back to their heavenly home, having received all of the essential ordinances of eternal exaltation." [12]

Far from being an esoteric or peripheral doctrine, these quotes illustrate that church leaders have in recent years positioned the belief in Heavenly Father and Mother at the bedrock of the gospel message. They recognize how it shapes our understanding of life's purpose, relationships to one another and God, and humanity's ultimate destiny.

2. We do have revealed knowledge of a Heavenly Mother and it's more than just Her existence.

In October 1991, President Gordon B. Hinckley, then serving as a member of the First Presidency under President Ezra Taft Benson, expressed that we have no revealed knowledge of Heavenly Mother. After quoting a prior address of his censuring prayer to Heavenly Mother, President Hinckley added to his remarks that "none of us can add to or diminish the glory of Her [Heavenly Mother] of whom we have no revealed knowledge." [13] His address suggested that our knowledge of Heavenly Mother was built on the hymn from Sister Eliza R. Snow, and as an outgrowth of logic or reasoning from gospel principles.

Since the publication of "A Mother There" and related Gospel Topics essays, the historical record became clearer, and President Hinckley's statement was tempered recently. In 2022, Elder Dale G. Renlund said affirmatively that "The doctrine of a Heavenly Mother comes by revelation." [14] This position aligned with historical precedents set by church leaders before President Hinckley. [15] While Elder Renlund admitted that very little has been revealed, he noted that what we do know is summarized in the Gospel Topics essay on the matter. Rather than merely refer members to that Gospel Topics essay, he called out some of what was known in his conference talk: our inherited divine nature from Heavenly Parents, and our aspiration to be like Them.

> **None of us can add to or diminish the glory of Her.**

Similarly, a church periodical article in the March 2017 New Era on "Why don't we know much about our Heavenly Mother?" articulated that while much has not been revealed, we do know "the role of our Heavenly Parents in working together for the salvation and exaltation of Their children." [16] They "want us to become like Them." Minimalist as though they may be, these now "rare and precious truths" are a meaningful advance away from the trajectory of earlier discourse that positioned Her as a celestial footnote, suggesting that a core nucleus about the doctrine of Heavenly Mother is forming.

As the belief in Heavenly Mother is acknowledged and explored, there's also been an effort to teach it carefully. For one, the Church has published the aforementioned Gospel Topics essays on both Heavenly Mother and Heavenly Parents. [17] Secondly, Elder Ballard advised religious educators to approach lesser-known and possibly misunderstood doctrines, like Heavenly Mother, with care [18] Young missionaries need to be "spiritually inoculated," given thoughtful and accurate presentations of church doctrine before they go out into the world.

He urged religious educators to study the official essays on Heavenly Mother and Heavenly Parents for proper context, and proceeded to elucidate several meaningful gospel principles arising from this cherished LDS belief and that of eternal marriage. Elder Renlund also urged members to be careful with speculating about the core teachings we have on Heavenly Mother for fear of "looking beyond the mark," and cautioned once more that church members refrain from praying to Heavenly Mother, as President Hinckley did. [19]

3. Heavenly Mother shares divine qualities and responsibilities alongside Heavenly Father in guiding Their children.

While church leaders continue to emphasize how we are born of Heavenly Parents and share a divine heritage from Them, there is a continued trend of expanding Heavenly Mother's roles outside of spirit birth. Elder Dieter F. Uchtdorf's conference addresses get us to consider Her divinity and Her shared responsibility with the Father over existence. In October 2017, Elder Uchtdorf told women and girls, "Remember that you are of the royal house of the kingdom of God, daughters of Heavenly Parents, who reign throughout the universe." [20] The prior year, Elder Uchtdorf described both our Heavenly Parents as "divine, immortal, and omnipotent." [21] The latter has not been an adjective commonly applied to Heavenly Mother [22]

Other church leaders have also addressed this topic. Elder Ballard emphasized that the plan of salvation was designed by both Heavenly Parents, extending Heavenly Mother's creative role beyond humanity's spiritual genesis and towards its divine becoming.[23] Her divine influence in our lives flows from Her love for us. As Elder Gary E. Stevenson explained, "A basic gospel principle is that we are children of loving Heavenly Parents. It is only natural for Them to help us in every way to return to our heavenly home." [24] Elder Stevenson noted that we can receive this help through spiritual impressions that guide us through life's challenges.

> **Elder Dieter F. Uchtdorf's conference addresses get us to consider Her divinity and Her shared responsibility with the Father over existence.**

Elder Ian S. Ardern, President in the Pacific Area Presidency, shared another means by which our Heavenly Parents bless us now: They send us warmth to strengthen us in our trials and as we make good decisions, aware of the difficulty of our mortal journey. Ardern explained, "I am, as you are, a beloved child of Heavenly Parents who care for us and who want us to succeed in our journey through mortality.

They knew from the beginning that the journey would be demanding, and They also knew that it needs to be that way for us to grow and to become more like our Saviour. At all times, and especially in those moments of desperation, we can feel the warmth of loving Heavenly Parents. An added warmth comes as we make and keep sacred covenants." [25]

4. Great focus has been made on the love of our Heavenly Parents for us.

Church leaders are more intentionally calling out the love of Heavenly Parents. [26] Elder Uchtdorf stressed: "My dear sisters in the gospel, whether you are 8 or 108, there is one thing that I hope you truly understand and know: You are loved. You are dear to your Heavenly Parents." [27]

They "truly love us," Elder Ulisses Soares emphasized. [28] Their love didn't belong only to the premortal realm, as Elder Ballard added that They "continue to love us now." [29] But nothing expresses this trend more than the revised Young Women's Theme, which is repeated by girls throughout church meeting houses every week:

5. The Atonement of Jesus Christ, with the associated ordinances of the priesthood, facilitates the reunion with our Heavenly Parents.

While articulating the joy of a homecoming with Heavenly Parents, church leaders have forged a tight link between that reunion and the first principles and ordinances of the gospel. The Atonement of Christ is central to this reunion, as Elder Ballard positioned Christ as "the hinge point that connects it all." [31] President Russell M. Nelson described the Savior himself as inviting us to follow "the covenant path back home to our Heavenly Parents and be with those we love." [32] This underscores that Christ is not only our guide but also the essential means by which we can return to our divine family. Most eloquently, Elder Holland testified, "In this and every hour [Jesus Christ] is, with nail-scarred hands, extending to us that same grace, holding on to us and encouraging us, refusing to let us go until we are safely home in the embrace of Heavenly Parents." [33]

> **Elder Ballard positioned Christ as "the hinge point that connects it all."**

Priesthood power plays a vital role in this process of sanctification and returning to our Heavenly Parents. As Elder Ballard explained, the "primary purpose of this priesthood power is to bless, sanctify, and purify us so we can live together with our families in the presence of our Heavenly Parents forever." [34] The ordinances performed through the priesthood — particularly in temples — are essential for unlocking the blessings of eternal life.

Elder Stevenson expressed that without the restoration of priesthood authority and keys, we would lack the necessary "vehicle" to return to our Heavenly Parents, making the priesthood fundamental to our spiritual journey. [35]

These teachings collectively emphasize that the Atonement of Christ, priesthood ordinances, and gospel principles are intricately woven together, providing a path to sanctification and a reunion with our Heavenly Parents. Each element plays a crucial role in this eternal plan, with Christ's love and sacrifice at the heart of it all.

The discourse on Heavenly Mother in the years following the publication of "A Mother There" reflects a nuanced yet deliberate expansion of pre-existing doctrinal themes, a deepening of the comfort with and articulation of ideas that have long circulated within LDS thought. Nonetheless, there also appears to be a growing confidence in discussing Heavenly Parents as a cohesive, loving partnership in the salvation of Their children, present to us to a small extent now, yet ultimately and fully reachable through the Son. Church leaders appear to be offering an exegesis on established truths, allowing for a more explicit recognition of previously expressed doctrines on behalf of the LDS church membership.

Notes and resources

[1] We expanded beyond the first historical survey of belief in a Heavenly Mother, which was published in 1987.

See Wilcox, Linda P., "The Mormon Concept of a Mother in Heaven," in Maureen Ursenbach Beecher, Lavina Fielding Anderson (eds.), Sisters in Spirit: Mormon Women in Historical and Cultural Perspective, Urbana: University of Illinois Press, 1987, p.64-77.

[2] Paulsen, David L.; Pulido, Martin. "A Mother There: A Survey of Historical Teachings about Mother in Heaven." BYU Studies 50.1 (January 2011), 70-97.

[3] "A Mother There," 4-6.

[4] What follows is a survey of some of the materials found since the publication of the original "A Mother There."

Heavenly Wife and Parent. A valiant defense of the church's theological position on

Heavenly Parents was elaborated by Elder B. H. Roberts, while serving as President of God, particularly that of Heavenly Mother. Roberts quotes Eliza R. Snow's poem and expresses that just as scripture presents a father to our spirits, we present a mother of them as well. "Now observe the peculiar position of these critics: It is all right for Jesus to have a mother; but it is all wrong for him to have a [physical, embodied] father. On the other hand, it is all right for men's spirits to have a Father in heaven, but our reviewers object to our doctrine of their having a mother there. ...I am puzzled to classify your views, or the kind of beings with which you people heaven. There seems to be objection in the review to the idea of the marriage relation existing in heaven and subsisting between divine beings. Loud complaint is made, if you hold that the intelligences of heaven obey the law of marriage. But who instituted marriage? God. And is it holy? You'll say God instituted something holy. If it is holy, how do you make it unholy for divine personages to practice? Is it not just as good for divine personages as for you imperfect men? Can it be that your ideas of the relationship of the sexes are so impure that you must needs regard that association as so unholy as to be unworthy of divine beings?" Roberts goes on to mention that the contemporary author praises marriage peopling and preserving the world and heaven. "Now, you prate to us about our belief, or the belief of some of us at least, that divine personages are in this holy relationship." But to Roberts, it is clear that no force within man's experience is so beneficial to him than marriage. See Improvement Era 10.9.702-708. See also Roberts' earlier A New Witness For God, 461-462. "What a revelation is here! As I have remarked elsewhere, instead of the God-given power of pro-creation being one of the chief things that is to pass away, it is one of the chief means of man's exaltation and glory in that great eternity, which like an endless vista stretches out before him!" "Instead of the commandment, 'Be fruitful, and multiply and replenish the earth,' being an unrighteous law, it is one by means of which the race of the Gods is perpetuated, and is as holy and pure as the commandment, 'Repent and be baptized.'"

Orson F. Whitney was most express on our Heavenly Parents being a pair and not an androgynous being, as later LDS writers have speculated. In 1929, he gave an example of the letter of scripture requiring interpretation by the spirit. He brought up Genesis 1:27 and observed, "To the casual reader this might imply that God is both male and female – a bi-sexual [androgynous] being. But we know better, having been correctly taught." God is an exalted man who sits enthroned in the heavens. Males are in the likeness of the Father, but "It was in the image or likeness of the Eternal Mother that woman was created. The Creator was speaking of man in the generic sense – mankind – when He said, 'Let us make man in our image, after our likeness.'" It is only "wedded, they are as one, the two together constituting the unit of the race." [See "The Letter and the Spirit" in RSM 26.4.176 (April 1929).] Franklin D. Richards likewise expressed that "Man, in his fullness, is a two-fold organization – male and female. Either being incapable of filling the measure of their creation alone, it requires the union of the two to complete man in the image of God." [See Course of Study for the Quorums of the Priesthood - Teachers, First Year, page 41. 1909.] It is when we enter the temple and enter into the eternal marriage covenant that we bring the greatest honor to our earthly and Heavenly parents in echoing their way of life. [See Hunter, Milton R. "The Fifth Commandment for Us." The Instructor 92.7 (July 1957), 201.]

Leaders in the 1940s continued to assert that we are the spiritual offspring of Heavenly Parents. [See "Our Homes" in Relief Society Magazine 27.12.802-8 (October 3, 1940). See Milton R. Hunter (First Council of Seventy) in "Man and His Destiny" Millennial Star 109.8.251. (August 1947); Eldred G. Smith (Patriarch to the Church) in "How Near to God are You?" in IE 61.6 (June 1958), 420-421; Henry D. Taylor in "Be Ye Therefore Perfect" (April 6, 1967); Russ Ballard in "The Hope of Eternal Life" in The Instructor 105.7.238 (July 1970).]

A Divine Person. In Women of the Mormon Church, Susa Young Gates (a church leader who served in both the YWMIA and Relief Society) and Leah D. Widtsoe (Susa's daughter and wife of apostle John A. Widtsoe) express the belief of Latter-day Saints "that they have both a heavenly Father and Mother from whose divine Home they were sent here on earth to learn, by faith, the lessons of mortal life. If worthy, we shall return in honor to our Heavenly Parents and partake of their glory" (emphasis added). [See Smith, Douglas H. and Smith, Barbara B. "Grandparenting and the Eternal Family Pattern." Religious Educator: Perspectives on the Restored Gospel 6, no. 2 (2005), 21. Douglas H. Smith is a former member of the Second Quorum of the Seventy. Barbara B. Smith is a former general president of the Relief Society. "What a breathtaking heritage: our spirit Father and Mother are Gods!"]

The divinity of Heavenly Parents was described commonly as a springboard for humanity's divine potential, as Their spirit children. Susa Young Gates shared in 1918 that she "possesses in embryo all that made Mother Eve, as well as our Heavenly Mother, good, gracious, and divine. Beauty, gifts, graces, which woman has or may possess, lie within my own soul as embryonic leaves in a calyx ready to open and bloom whenever my will calls them forth." She notes that her religion "proves to me the divine equality of the sexes and of various peoples." [See Susa Young Gates in "What my Faith Means to Me" in Juvenile Instructor, 53.6.291.]

Before being ordained as an apostle, in 1892 Orson F. Whitney spoke at a unitarian conference in Salt Lake City, and expressed that latter-day saints hold "that men and women are literally the sons and daughters of Deity; that we [have] a Mother as well as a Father in Heaven, and that we men and women are in their image or likeness, male, and female. And is it not reasonable to expect that the child will develop to the status of the Parent? We are divine beings in embryo, and it is onlya question of time when we shall blossom in perfection, and be like our Father and Mother in heaven."

[5] Foreign articles show that the LDS doctrine of a Heavenly Mother was taught in various European countries, Brazil and South Africa. See Imbeck, Emma. "Mein Kind, bewahre die Gebote deines Vaters und hass nicht fahren das Gesetz deiner Mutter" in Der Stern 51.20.313-314 (October 15, 1919); Anderson, Haldis. "Vaarkonferansen I Trondhjem" Morgenstjernen 4.9.137-138 (May 1, 1925); Lillywhite, John P. "Moeder, Huis en Hemel" (Mother, Home and Heaven) in De Ster 32.9 (1 May 1927); Donald, Don Mac. "Editorial: Heavenly Father and Mother" in Cumorah's Southern Messenger 8.4.58-59 (April 20, 1934); Howells, Rulon Stanley (Mission President). "Editorial" in A Gaivota 11.8 (August 1949); Provost, Sterling R. "Songs in Their Hearts" in Cumorah's Southern Messenger 26.2.25 (February 1951); Sister Van de Put (from the central board of the genealogical society). "De Utrechtse Districts-Conferentie" in De Ster no. 12 (December 1960); During the Utrecht District Conference in October 23-24 1965, President Van Rij commented on the hymn, "O My Father" in "De Utrechtse Districtsconferentie op 24 oktober" in De Ster no. 11 (November 1965); Eberhard, Ernest, Jr. "Wie man Nichtmitgliedern in seiner Familie hilft" in Der Stern 103.11.39 (November 1977); Sluter, Rita in the Forum of De Ster (No. 10, October 1991), "Hoe u zelfvertrouwen kunt ntwikkelen, terwijl u toch op de Heer blijft vertrouwen."

Some express the appeal of the doctrine to converts. See Schwarz aus Barmen, Helene. "Frei vom Irrtum." Der Stern 48.17.268-269 (September 1, 1916). Or how it comforted those with the death of a loved one. See West, Orson B. (editor, Mission President) in Skandinaviens Stjerne (April 1945), 54-55.

[6] Dove Song: Heavenly Mother in Mormon Poetry. Eds. Chadwick, Tyler; Patterson, Dayna; Pulido, Martin. El Cerrito, CA: Peculiar Pages, 2018. The church's official Gospel Topics essay on "Heavenly Mother" still reflects dated scholarship that "The earliest published references to the doctrine appeared shortly after Joseph Smith's death in 1844, in documents written by his close associates." In fact, William W. Phelps published a reference to the doctrine in February 1844, roughly four months before Joseph Smith's death, in the very periodical Joseph Smith edited, the Times and Seasons. Phelps later attributed this belief just months after the Prophet's death in his hymn, "A Voice From the Prophet: Come to Me," which was sung at the dedication of the Seventies Hall in Nauvoo. This hymn has Joseph introducing thesaints to a Mother in heaven, the queen. This is covered in detail in Dove Song, 31-34; 341-344.

[7] Church leaders, for instance, reference us being taught by our Heavenly Mother in the premortal realm. [See Ashton, Brian K. "The Father." October 2018 general conference.] They continue to note our ability to become like our Heavenly Parents. [See D. Todd Christofferson. "The Divine Plan of Becoming More." For the Strength of Youth, July 2021; Jean B. Bingham "Extraordinary Daughters of God." BYU Women's Conference address given May 5, 2017.]

Elder Jeffrey R. Holland gave glowing praise to mothers everywhere, including Heavenly Mother, thanking them for "shaping souls, for forming character, and for demonstrating the pure love of Christ. ... for your crucial role in fulfilling the purposes of eternity." [Holland, Jeffrey R. "Behold Thy Mother." October 2015 general conference.]

Church leaders continue to promote that this doctrine enables us to be more unified and appreciate other human beings as our spiritual siblings. It empowers us to see them from an eternal perspective and be less judgmental. It allows us to see the human family as one, to act fairly and serve one another. Most expressly, Elder William K. Jackson explained: "This culture espouses the concept of equal worth. There is no recognition of caste or class. We are, after all, brothers and sisters, spirit children of our Heavenly Parents—literally. There is no prejudice or "us versus them" mentality in the greatest of all cultures. We are all "us." We are all "them." We believe that we are responsible and accountable for ourselves, one another, the Church, and our world." [See Jackson, William K. "The Culture of Christ." October 2020 general conference. See also: "Children of Heavenly Parents." Harkness, Lisa L. Friend, September 2020; "Judging Righteous Judgment (Even on Social Media)." Young Women general board members and Liahona staff, Liahona, December 2020; Taylor, Brian K. "Am I Child of God?" May 2018 general conference.]

Earthly parenthood serves as a key to understanding and developing Heavenly Parenthood. Elder M. Russell Ballard emphasized that Saints must "understand that the purpose of mortality is to become more like God by gaining physical bodies, exercising agency, and assuming roles that previously belonged only to Heavenly Parents—roles of husband, wife, and parent." Through these roles, we mirror the divine family structure, transitioning from being children to becoming parents ourselves. [See Ballard, "By Study and by Faith", 9.] In marriage, sexual intimacy and procreation play an essential role in this process, as they allow us to experience aspects of Heavenly Parenthood. [See Renlund, Dale G., and Renlund, Ruth Lybbert. "The Divine Purposes of Sexual Intimacy." Ensign. August 2020.]

As parents, we are called to lead and protect our families, much like our Heavenly Parents. Family councils, for instance, offer a way to guide and safeguard our homes, reflecting divine stewardship. [See Ballard, M. Russell. "Family Councils." April 2016 general conference.] Elder Richard G. Scott emphasized the lasting nature of this responsibility, stating that "in time we will be released from all other assignments we receive but not from that of father and mother." Parenthood, then, is not just an earthly role, but an eternal one that deepens our connection to and understanding of our Heavenly Parents' divine work. [See Scott, Richard G. "He Lives! All Glory to His Name!" April 2010 general conference.] President Oaks stated, "As spirits, we desired to achieve the eternal life enjoyed by our heavenly parents. At that point we had progressed as far as we could without a mortal experience in a physical body." [See Dallin H. Oaks. "The Great Plan." April 2020 general conference.]

[8] Oaks, Dallin H. "Apostasy and Restoration," Ensign, May 1995, 87. For a more recent affirmation of this, see Oaks, Dallin H. "No Other Gods." October 2013 general conference.

[9] Holland, Jeffrey R. "The Message, The Meaning, and the Multitude." October 2019 general conference.

[10] Rasband, Ronald A. "Lest Thou Forget." October 2016 general conference.

[11] Ballard, M. Russell. "To Whom Shall We Go?" October 2016 general conference.

[12] Ballard, M. Russell. "The Essential Role of Women." BYU Women's Conference address given May 1, 2015. See also, for similar points brought up in Ballard, M. Russell. "By Study and by Faith." Religious Educator: Perspectives on the Restored Gospel 17, no. 3 (2016): 8.

[13] Hinckley, Gordon B. "Daughters of God." October 1991 general conference.

[14] Renlund, Dale G. "Your Divine Nature and Eternal Destiny." April 2022 general conference.

[15] Precedents include but are not limited to these instances: Joseph F. Smith (Second Counselor in the First Presidency under Wilford Woodruff, first assistant in the Young men presidency) in "Discourse Delivered at the Oneida Stake" in Deseret News (February 9, 1895), shared that Eliza R. Snow's poem caused no stir in 1845 because the doctrine was not a foreign one. He argued history shows the concept originated with Joseph Smith, revealed to him from God. A year later, George Q. Cannon (First Counselor in the First Presidency, superintendent of the Deseret Sunday School Union) in General Conference in "The False Theories of Man" stated that the truths of Snow's poem (Heavenly Mother) were revealed through Joseph Smith. In 1877, Eliza R. Snow edited the Women of Mormondom while serving as the second Relief Society general president, which expressed LDS belief in a Heavenly Mother as a revelation stemming from the Prophet Joseph Smith. Bishop Heber C. Iverson in a 1908 General Conference explained that the belief in a Heavenly Mother was ridiculed 70 years before when announced in this hymn, teaching what first was revealed to Joseph. [See Conference Report, April 1908, Second Overflow Meeting, 70-71.]

[See also Joseph A. McRae (Editor, former President of the Colorado and Western States mission) in "A Tribute to the Memory of the Prophet of the Last Dispensation, Joseph Smith" in Liahona: The Elders' Journal 9.26.409; John A. Widtsoe (Apostle) in "Woman in the Church" in Millennial Star 90.11.169; John A. Widtsoe in "Everlasting Motherhood" in MStar 90.298; Susa Young Gates (former church leader, Mormon writer) and Leah D. Widtsoe (her daughter, wife of John A. Widtsoe) The Life Story of Brigham Young, 295; Elder Milton R. Hunter (First Council of the Seventy) Conference Report, October 1945, Afternoon Meeting, 108.]

[16] "Why don't we know much about our Heavenly Mother?" New Era, March 2017.

[17] "Mother in Heaven." churchofjesuschrist.org/study/manual/gospel-topics-essays/mother-in-heaven; "Heavenly Parents." churchofjesuschrist.org/study/manual/gospel-topics/heavenly-parents

[18] Ballard, "By Study and by Faith," 8-9.

[19] Renlund, "Your Divine Nature and Eternal Destiny."

[20] Uchtdorf, Dieter F. "Three Sisters." October 2017 general conference.

[21] Uchtdorf, Dieter F. "O How Great the Plan of Our God!" October 2016 general conference.

[22] In fact, in 1895, George Q. Cannon was disturbed at the suggestion of Emmeline B. Wells, who had promoted writings from Elizabeth Cady Stanton, that Heavenly Mother could be "equal in power and glory with the masculine." [See Cannon, George Q. (First Counselor in the First Presidency, superintendent of the Deseret Sunday School Union) in Juvenile Instructor 30.314-17.]

[23] Ballard, M. Russell. "The Eternal Importance of Family." Address delivered on October 27, 2015 at the ninth World Congress of Families held in Salt Lake City, Utah. Published in the Ensign, January 2018.

[24] Stevenson, Gary E. "Blessings of a Gospel Perspective." BYU-Hawaii devotional, September 19, 2017.

[25] Ardern, Ian S. "The Warmth of the Gospel." Liahona, June 2021.

[26] "I want you to know that your Heavenly Parents love you very much. They want the best for you." Martinez, Hugo E. "He Wants the Best for Me." Friend, February 2019. "Our Heavenly Parents love us, Their children." Aburto, Reyna I. "Part of an Eternal Family." Liahona, September 2020.

[27] Uchtdorf, Dieter F. "Living the Gospel Joyful." October 2014 general conference.

[28] Soares, Ulisses. "Brothers and Sisters in Christ." October 2023 general conference

[29] Ballard, M. Russell. "Giving Our Spirits Control Over Our Bodies." October 2019 general conference.

[30] Cordon, Bonnie H. "Beloved Daughters." October 2019 general conference.

[31] Ballard, "By Study and By Faith," 8.

[32] Nelson, Russell M. "Come, Follow Me." April 2019 general conference. See also Nelson, Russell M. "Joy and Spiritual Survival." October 2016 general conference; Uchtdorf, Dieter F. "God Among Us." April 2021 general conference.

[33] Holland, Jeffrey R. "Be Ye Therefore Perfect - Eventually." October 2017 general conference.

[34] Ballard, M. Russell. "This is My Work and My Glory." April 2013 general conference.

[35] Stevenson, Gary E. "Where Are the Keys and Authority of the Priesthood?" April 2016 general conference. Alongside the covenants and ordinances, Elder Ulisses Soares reminds us that our thoughts, words, and actions must align with divine principles if we hope to reach the "level of the divinity of our Heavenly Parents." See also Ulisses Soares. "Abide in the Lord's Territory!" April 2012 general conference.

This intimates that living the gospel and keeping our covenants isn't just a matter of compliance but a transformative process that elevates us toward divine nature, preparing us for eternal life in the presence of our Heavenly Parents.

See also "Keep Paddling!," Oaks, Dallin H. Friend, September 2018; "Be of Good Cheer." Oaks, Dallin H. October 2020 general conference; Uchtdorf, Dieter F. "O How Great the Plan of Our God!" October 2016 general conference; Bingham, Jean B. "United in Accomplishing God's Work." April 2020 general conference.

STUDY HELPS
A Mother There

"Mother in Heaven" Gospel Topics essay footnotes

Footnote 2,3: "'A Mother There': A Survey of Historical Teachings About Mother in Heaven," BYU Studies 50: 1 (2011), p. 70-97. By David L. Paulsen and Martin Pulido.

Footnote 5: "The Significance of 'O My Father' in the Personal Journey of Eliza R. Snow," BYU Studies 36: 1 (1996), p. 84-126. By Jill Mulvay Derr.

Study 1

Genesis 1:26-27; Psalms 82:6; Romans 8:16-17; ; Moses 3:4-7

What do you learn from these scriptures about Heavenly Mother?

What changes when you understand that Heavenly Mother was involved in the creation of the earth and all things in it? Does this change how you view women? How?

Has your thinking changed about Heavenly Mother as you have learned about Her? Explain how. Do you feel any different about yourself or your earthly mother? How?

Study 2

The last phrase of the third verse in "O My Father" says: "I've a Mother there," setting forth the principle of Heavenly Mother's existence. When you think of this phrase, how does it feel to know She is there?

What is your "personal vision" of what attributes Heavenly Mother has? (Tip: footnote number 2 has lots of information on this!)

Study 3

> You sisters, I suppose have read the poem which my sister composed many years ago, and which is sung quite frequently now in our meetings. It tells us that we not only have a father in that high and glorious place but that we have a mother too, and you will become as great as your mother if you are faithful. – President Lorenzo Snow

What have you learned about this greatness of our Mother that you can become?

Has the song, "O My Father" been an influence in your thoughts about Heavenly Mother? If so, in what way?

Suggested Reading

"Departure and Reunion", Becky Edwards, *Cherish* book 1, p. 123
"Someone Watching Over Me," Jared Buhler, *Cherish* book 1, p. 126
"Untitled", Autumn Nelson, *Cherish* book 1, p. 139
"The World is Crying For a Mother," Ashli Carnicelli, *Cherish* book 1, p. 111

Teachings of Lorenzo Snow, editor Clyde Williams, (Bookcraft, 1998) p. 7.

5. SIDE BY SIDE

"Susa Young Gates, a prominent leader in the Church, wrote in 1920 that Joseph Smith's visions and teachings revealed the truth that 'the divine Mother, [is] **side by side** with the divine Father."

Mother in Heaven essay, paragraph 3

PARTNERSHIP

The Gospel Topics essay, "Mother in Heaven," is clear that men and women are to be equal partners in family relationships. Elder Ulisses Soares expounds:

> The restored gospel of Jesus Christ proclaims the principle of full partnership between woman and man, both in mortal life and in the eternities. ... Let us consider fundamental principles that strengthen the partnership between man and woman. The first principle is that we are all alike unto God. According to gospel doctrine, the difference between woman and man does not override the eternal promises that God has for His sons and daughters. One has no greater possibilities for celestial glory than the other in the eternities. The Savior Himself invites all of us, God's children, "to come unto him and partake of his goodness; and he denieth none that come unto him." (2 Nephi 26:33) Therefore, in this context, we are all considered equal before Him.
>
> When spouses understand and incorporate this principle, they do not position themselves as president and vice president of their family. There is no superiority or inferiority in the marriage relationship, and neither walks ahead of or behind the other. They walk side by side, as equals, the divine offspring of God. They become one in thought, desire, and purpose, leading and guiding the family unit together.

Church leaders also confirm that men and women working within their quorums and organizations as equal partners is the most effective way to conduct the work of the Lord. President Jean B. Bingham addressed this in April 2020 general conference: "When women and men work together, we accomplish a great deal more than we do working separately."

Restored gospel truth helps us eradicate erroneous models — one of which is how people interact with each other. There should be no arrogance or superiority of any gender identity over another, no suppression of someone unlike ourselves. Zion is to be of one heart and one mind of purpose, living and working in unity. The restored knowledge of a Mother in Heaven makes this relationship clear.

Ulisses Soares, "In Partnership With the Lord," October 2022 general conference.
Jean B. Bingham, Relief Society general president, 2017-22, "United in Accomplishing God's Work," April 2020 general conference.

PARTNERSHIP IN MARRIAGE
Roger and Anne Pimentel

When we first got married, we never talked about who would work and who would stay at home.

It was always just... understood that Roger would pursue a career and be the breadwinner, and Anne would stay at home with the kids once they came along. And that's what we did. Roger started a career, got a masters degree along the way, and moved our family to different states to follow job changes. Anne gave birth to four boys – not all at once – and took on an outsized load of the feeding and changing while Roger was at the office.

> *As we've learned more about our Heavenly Mother and the eternal marriage relationship of our Heavenly Parents, we've gotten away from traditional roles in marriage, too. Instead, we're trying to make our marriage reflect the relationship we believe our Heavenly Parents have.*

There's nothing remarkable about this marriage and parenting arrangement; especially in the Church, and especially in the suburban United States where we both grew up, this is the dominant separation of duties. Even *The Family: A Proclamation to the World* spells out these roles, where the father "provide[s] the necessities of life" and the mother focuses on the "nurture of their children." These gender roles are, for sure, deeply embedded in our Latter-day Saint culture.

But as we've gotten older, we've drifted away from gender norms. One of us bakes bread, the other played in a city sports league. One of us is artistic, the other is analytical. One of us is the president of an organization, the other plays the piano. And in each of these juxtapositions, each person might not be the one of us you expect.

As we've learned more about our Heavenly Mother and the eternal marriage relationship of our Heavenly Parents, we've gotten away from traditional roles in marriage, too. Instead, we're trying to make our marriage reflect the relationship we believe our Heavenly Parents have. It's been said, and attributed to Maya Angelou, to "Do the best you can until you know better. Then when you know better, do better." We know better now. And we're committed, now, to do better.

SIDE BY SIDE

What kind of marriage relationship do our Heavenly Mother and Heavenly Father have? Do They have distinct roles? Does our Heavenly Father work a metaphorical 9-to-5, the breadwinner for His eternal family, while our Heavenly Mother tends to the children? Does Heavenly Father have the final say in making decisions? It can feel like They perform different functions; we pray to and worship our Heavenly Father, while being inaccurately taught, in hushed tones, that we shouldn't talk about our Heavenly Mother.

> **Not only did our Heavenly Parents work side by side before this life, but They continue to do so as we fumble our way through lives where we have forgotten everything and rely on imperfect knowledge of Them.**

But this is not the picture of our Heavenly Parents that has been revealed through Church leaders in this dispensation. We aren't taught about a submissive female partner to our Heavenly Father. We aren't taught male headship. Instead, the Heavenly Mother we know has been "side by side" with the Father in major theological events we read about in scripture. Our Heavenly Mother is in all places where decisions are being made. [1]

Our Heavenly Mother and Heavenly Father are co-creators; the "eternal Mother [is] the partner with the Father in the creation of worlds." [2] But not only are they co-creators of the Earth and the universe of physical creations, They are also the co-founders of the plan of salvation. Elder M. Russell Ballard described it as the "divine plan designed by Heavenly Parents who love us." [3] It's evocative to think of our Heavenly Mother seated next to our Heavenly Father —metaphorically, and perhaps also literally — as we gathered together in the great Council before this life, and as She "smiled on Her righteous children as they voted to uphold the will of the Council in Heaven and chose to come to earth." [4]

Not only did our Heavenly Parents work side by side before this life, but They continue to do so as we fumble our way through lives where we have forgotten everything and rely on imperfect knowledge of Them. We're taught, of course, to develop a relationship with our Heavenly Father. But there's no doubt that our Heavenly Mother is there too. Susa Young Gates, the daughter of Brigham Young and an influential figure in the early church, talked about our Heavenly Mother keeping an eye of "watchful care" over us and giving "careful training" as we move throughout our lives. [5] For some people, this echoes the loving, nurturing roles they associate with their earthly mothers. For others, this is a supporting, strengthening presence they have never known.

SIDE BY SIDE

President Harold B. Lee taught this truth: "We forget that we have a Heavenly Father and a Heavenly Mother who are even more concerned, probably, than our earthly father and mother, and that influences from beyond are constantly working to try to help us when we do all we can." [6] Elder Jeffrey R. Holland, then the President of BYU, asked that if as mortal parents we "can love so much and try so hard, what does that say of a more Godly love that differs from our own as the stars differ from the sun? On a particularly difficult day, ... what would this world's inhabitants pay to know that Heavenly Parents are reaching across those same streams and mountains and deserts, anxious to hold them close?" [7]

What do we learn from this divine relationship, that we can model our marriages after?

As much as our culture has taught us that men and women — and by association, husbands and wives — can only play certain roles in family relationships, prophets and apostles have recently been vocal to the opposite effect. Elder Ulisses Soares verified that husbands and wives "do not position themselves as president or vice president of their family. ... There is no superiority or inferiority in the marriage relationship, and neither walks ahead of or behind the other. They walk side by side, as equals, the divine offspring of God." [8] Could it be any different with our Heavenly Parents? Should we strive for anything different?

> **What does it mean to be "side by side" as partners in a marriage? If our Heavenly Parents have operated literally side by side, does that mean we need to do all the same things at the same time?**

President Thomas S. Monson used that same "side by side" phrase when speaking to the men of the Church in general conference: "Your wife is your equal. In marriage neither partner is superior nor inferior to the other. You walk side by side as a son and a daughter of God." [9] Elder Quentin L. Cook beats the same drum, emphasizing the "side by side" ideal in marriages: "Wives are equal to their husbands. Marriage requires a full partnership where wives and husbands work side by side to meet the needs of the family." [10]

So, what does this mean practically? What does it mean to be "side by side" as partners in a marriage? If our Heavenly Parents have operated literally side by side, does that mean we need to do all the same things at the same time? Do husband and wife need to both work outside the home, and both pick up the kids from school, and both make dinner? Of course not. The example They set for us is not about specific behaviors, but rather about the approach.

Having a marriage relationship modeled after that of our Heavenly Parents means being intentional. It means not defaulting to cultural norms just for the sake of doing so.

In our marriage, it has meant being intentional in talking about how Anne never had the opportunity to grow a career early in our marriage. It has meant both of us stepping into new roles, as Anne helps to run a non-profit organization and Roger takes a newfound interest in making bread (okay, we'll reveal those two). It has meant being side by side — not that we do every single thing together, but neither is a step ahead or a step behind.

Being side by side and working together means making decisions together. There's nothing wrong with a marriage where the husband works full-time and the wife takes a leading role in raising the children, if that's what you decide together to do. But a side-by-side marriage provides space and encouragement for the wife to do things that expand her soul and help her feel whole. It relieves the husband of the weight of all the decision-making, and encourages the development of healthy, caring, and complete relationships with their children. It tells the wife that bearing and raising children is not her sole purpose, and that she has value even when the children are grown. Being side by side means that both partners are their whole selves and live their fullest lives through — and this is the important part — making the decision to do so together.

Our Heavenly Parents have set the model for us. They co-created this world and co-founded the plan that sent us here. They continue to watch over us every single day, the way parents do. And They do it together. Side by side.

SOURCES

1 Referencing Ruth Bader Ginsburg, as quoted in "Ginsburg: Court needs another woman," USA Today, May 5, 2009, https://usatoday30.usatoday.com/news/washington/judicial/2009-05-05-ruthginsburg_N.htm.
2 Edward Tullidge, The Women of Mormondom (New York: Tullidge and Crandall, 1877), 193-94.
3 M. Russell Ballard, When Thou Art Converted: Continuing Our Search for Happiness (Salt Lake City: Deseret Book, 2001), 62.
4 Paulsen, David L. and Pulido, Martin (2011) "'A Mother There': A Survey of Historical Teachings about Mother in Heaven," BYU Studies Quarterly: Vol. 50 : Iss. 1, Article 7, 12. Referencing L[ula] L. Greene Richards, "A Thread of Thought," Woman's Exponent 29 (Aug 15 & Sept 1, 1900): 27.
5 Susa Young Gates, "In the Realm of Girlhood: Lesson V," Young Woman's Journal 17 (January 1906): 41.
6 Harold B. Lee, "The Influence and Responsibility of Women," Relief Society Magazine 51, no. 2 (February 1964): p. 85.
7 Jeffrey R. Holland, However Long and Hard the Road (Salt Lake City: Deseret Book, 1985), 47.
8 Ulisses Soares, "In Partnership with the Lord," October 2022 general conference.
9 Thomas S. Monson, "Priesthood Power," April 2011 general conference.
10 Quentin L. Cook, "LDS Women Are Incredible!," April 2011 general conference.

ON EQUAL PEDESTALS

J. Kirk Richards

SIDE BY SIDE

WHOLENESS AND TOGETHERNESS:
MODELING THE PATTERN OF HEAVENLY PARENTS

Amy Watkins Jensen

When I tell people I teach middle school, their faces often reflect a mix of horror and pity. They usually say something like, "You must be a saint." Yes, yes, I am a saint. And like all good saints, I'm a humble champion for a cause. My cause? The education of human beings during the most intense, volatile, odorous, fascinating, and wonderful phase of their development.

> *This strategy is incredibly effective because it fosters the continuous internalization of covenantal truths through individual practice.*

Admittedly, it's not an easy job. Middle schoolers, after all, are caught in a hormone-infused whirlwind of malodorous puberty. So yes, call me a saint. Hand me my halo and my roses — deserved or not — I'll take the title.

Honestly, being a saint isn't all that rare. I was born into sainthood, and maybe you were too. One lesson I've learned in my saintly pursuits as a middle school teacher also applies to my efforts as a member of The Church of Jesus Christ of Latter-day Saints, where we humbly and collectively champion the cause of Christ: good modeling is essential for creating a culture of learning and growth.

In my classroom, I often employ the "I do, we do, you do" teaching strategy. This involves demonstrating a concept (I do), guiding students as they practice (we do), and then allowing them to work independently (you do) to solidify their understanding. It's a strategy designed to move students from teacher-led instruction to independent mastery. It's modeling at its best because it supportively leads students toward internalizing and mastering concepts for themselves.

At church, we can use similar methods to make great strides in our collective journey toward Christ. In fact, it's a strategy I may have learned first as a missionary and later as a teacher in the Missionary Training Center. Show others what it looks like to follow Christ through your behaviors and actions (I do), invite them to study the gospel and participate in church activities with support (we do), and then encourage them to be baptized and apply gospel principles to their lives (you do).

This strategy is incredibly effective because it fosters the continuous internalization of covenantal truths through individual practice. But it all begins with effective modeling — without it, the entire strategy falls apart. Glorious truths will remain abstract if we fail to demonstrate them in action. This commitment to humility and openness in teaching parallels effective ways we model spiritual truths.

Interestingly, modern scientific research increasingly supports the wisdom of our doctrine of side-by-side leadership, revealing how collaboration and shared responsibilities foster stronger, more effective outcomes — both in the classroom and in spiritual growth. Rigorous research from Northwestern University confirms that flourishing comes through men and women working together. This aligns with our doctrine, which states, "Our theology begins with Heavenly Parents. Our highest aspiration is to be like them." Heavenly Parents working side by side is "the divine pattern established for us as children of Heavenly Parents." But do we consistently model this essential doctrine at church?

> By visibly and consistently modeling the collaborative leadership exemplified by our Heavenly Parents, we create an environment that reflects our doctrine and maximizes the collective strengths of men and women.

The Northwestern study on mixed-gender research teams underscores a vital truth: collaborative partnership between genders leads to innovation and impact. The researchers found that teams with gender-balanced ratios, particularly those close to 50:50, produced work that was significantly more novel and influential than that of same-gender teams. This finding is particularly relevant when applied to modeling leadership within the Church. Just as mixed-gender teams in science leverage unique perspectives and collaborative dynamics to achieve groundbreaking results, side-by-side leadership between men and women in Church settings could foster greater innovation and spiritual growth. By visibly and consistently modeling the collaborative leadership exemplified by our Heavenly Parents, we create an environment that reflects our doctrine and maximizes the collective strengths of men and women. The Church benefits when we use all our strength and talents to the building of Zion. When women and men model the essential truth of Heavenly Parents who work together for the benefit of Their children we foster a culture of balance, innovation, and flourishing for all Saints.

How can we better model the Divine pattern laid out for us by our expansive understanding of Deity? What can we do to seek alignment in practice with Doctrine? What can we do to align practices with doctrine?

SIDE BY SIDE

In a living gospel and a church in the midst of restoration, we need not be discouraged by what is, but can always find hope in the possibility of what may be. President Russell M. Nelson has done much to remind us that we are in a process of continuous restoration. During his tenure, he has embraced an almost "Marie Kondo" approach to examining our traditions and practices — doing away with the two-hour block, redefining our Church moniker, and insisting that women be called by their proper titles. The unveiling of women in the temple and other measures he has taken to make temple ordinances more egalitarian demonstrate that Church leadership values gender equality in institutional practices.

So, can we continue this movement? Can we carefully evaluate each practice, asking: Does this still "spark joy?" Does it align with doctrine and our discipleship of Jesus Christ? If a practice fosters partnership, unity, and wholeness, we keep it. If it no longer serves, we thank it for its role and gently set it aside.

And what about new practices — practices that place us on solid footing in our "I do, we do, you do" model of learning egalitarian discipleship? Can we imagine practices that reflect wholeness and encourage both women and men to bring their full selves to the body of Christ?

> **Can we carefully evaluate each practice, asking: Does this still "spark joy?" Does it align with doctrine and our discipleship of Jesus Christ?**

For instance, can we imagine a future where women on the stake council are counseled with when deciding on a stake president calling? How about a future where Relief Society presidents sit side by side with their male administrative counterparts on the stand? Could we make it a standard to include women leaders in every meeting where decisions affecting their stewardship are made? What if we invited women to participate in moves and encouraged men to cook meals for families in need? What if we recognized women's priesthood power with meaningful language and practices that confirm their spiritual authority? Could we affirm the importance of collaborative, united partnership by ensuring no leadership meeting occurs without women leaders present?

Might we do well to model our doctrine of Heavenly Parents who lead side by side, so that we can better internalize the truth that we are all alike unto God and that every part of the body of Christ is essential to the building of Zion? Would such modeling help us more easily and wholly knit ourselves together to become of one heart and one mind?

Ultimately, questions about wholeness and togetherness stem from faith in our doctrine, trust in prophetic love, and hope for the bright future of Zion.

> We must show, through both word and practice, what it means to work side by side as equals, as modeled by our Heavenly Parents.

Seeking alignment between doctrine and practice is not only valid but vital to our collective flourishing.

If we fail to model the side-by-side leadership so central to our theology, what balance and wholeness might remain out of reach?

In the end, whether in the classroom or the Church, the principles remain the same: effective modeling is essential for growth, learning, and flourishing. Just as my students rely on "I do, we do, you do" to move from guided practice to mastery, we as a Church must model the truths we proclaim. We must show, through both word and practice, what it means to work side by side as equals, as modeled by our Heavenly Parents. If middle schoolers can rise to the challenge of learning amidst the chaos of their development, surely we as saints can rise to the challenge of living in alignment with our doctrines. After all, sainthood isn't about perfection—it's about championing a cause greater than ourselves, modeling Christlike love, and working together to build Zion in all its fullness. So yes, call me a saint, and let's get to work.

SIDE BY SIDE

STUDY HELPS
Side By Side

"Mother in Heaven" Gospel Topics essay footnote

Footnote 7: "The Vision Beautiful," Improvement Era, April 1920, p. 542. By Susa Young Gates.

Study 1

> "Side: (n) either half of body; right or left; an aspect; a point of view; aimed towards one side; ally oneself." —Webster's Handy College Dictionary (1972, p.421)
>
> "Side by Side: (adj) beside another; in the same place; time or circumstances." —The Merriam-Webster Dictionary (2022, p.679)

What strikes you in these definitions about how our Heavenly Parents work together side by side?

How do you envision Heavenly Mother and Heavenly Father working side by side for the salvation of the human family?

Study 2

> Most Mormon leaders would not understand how Father and Mother could be divine alone. For either to be fully God, each must have a partner, with whom to share the power of endless lives. — "A Mother There," p.11

When you read the above statement, what and how does it make you feel?

What does the "power of endless lives" mean to you? Give a definition of the phrase.

List some activities that Heavenly Mother and Heavenly Father work hand in hand to accomplish.

SIDE BY SIDE

Study 3

Use your imagination to visualize Heavenly Mother and Heavenly Father working together side by side to create. What does your scenario look like?

How has your knowledge of Heavenly Mother and Heavenly Father working together side by side been an influence in the way you and your spouse fulfill this concept? How does it affect your relationship with others you come in contact with, such as family members or people you work with? How does this affect the way you serve at church?

Study 4

> Parenthood requires both father and mother, whether the creation of spirits in the premortal life or of physical tabernacles on earth. A Heavenly Mother shares parenthood with the Heavenly Father. This concept leaves Latter-day Saints to believe she is like him in glory, perfection, compassion, wisdom, and holiness. — Elaine A. Cannon

Why is it necessary for Heavenly Mother and Heavenly Father to work side by side?

Why is it important for earthly parents to work side by side? What can couples do to help them be successful in doing this?

Why is it important for church leaders to work side by side? What can a ward or stake council do to help them be successful in doing this?

Suggested Reading

"Partnership," Jill Freestone, *Cherish* book 2, p.189
"What My Heavenly Parents Have," Brittany Manjarrez, *Cherish* book 1, p.145

David L. Paulsen, Martin Pulido, "A Mother There: A Survey of Historical Teachings about Mother in Heaven," BYU Studies 50.1 (January 2011), 70-97.
Elaine Anderson Cannon, "Mother in Heaven," Encyclopedia of Mormonism (1992).

6. DIVINE NATURE AND DESTINY

"In The Family: A Proclamation to the World, issued in 1995,
the First Presidency and Quorum of the Twelve Apostles declared,
'Each [person] is a beloved son or daughter of Heavenly Parents,
and as such, each has a **divine nature and destiny**.'"

Mother in Heaven essay, paragraph 3

DIVINE NATURE AND DESTINY

THE VALUE OF DIVINE NATURE

For thirty-six years, generations of Latter-day Saint girls focused on the Young Women Values: faith, divine nature, faith, divine nature, individual worth, choice and accountability, good works, integrity, and virtue. President Ardeth G. Kapp was inspired in 1983 to update the Personal Progress program with the Values as the foundation. Young women of the Church needed a vision for who they could become throughout their lives.

What was President Kapp's vision that made it important for thousands of young women to sear them into their minds and hearts? If you were one of those Young Women, how do the Values affect your life now? How did they help you in decisions about higher education, who to marry, how to raise children, how you allow your spouse to treat you? What do the Values mean in your interactions with the people of your community, and the names on the screen you interact with via the internet? Why did it matter that President Kapp wanted everyone to repeat the Values in every Young Women meeting?

> *The most important things for us to see clearly are who God is and who we really are — sons and daughters of Heavenly Parents, with a divine nature and eternal destiny.*
> —Sister Michelle D. Craig

For that matter, how are men impacted by the knowledge that we all have a divine nature? The Values, at their core, were not just for girls. They are the attributes and traits that all people, regardless of gender, should develop to become more like the Savior, more like our Heavenly Parents.

When the Young Women theme was rewritten in 2019 by President Bonnie H. Cordon, the phrasing changed from "daughters of Heavenly Father" to "daughters of Heavenly Parents," bringing our Mother in Heaven into further visibility for girls, strengthening faith and reinforcing testimony of our divine nature and individual worth.

The Gospel Topics essay, "Mother in Heaven," reiterates the value of Divine Nature and keeps it emblazoned on our hearts.

Laurel Christensen Day, "The inspiring truth about Ardeth Kapp I want to shout from the rooftops," LDS Living, April 8, 2024, www.ldsliving.com/the-inspiring-truth-about-ardeth-kapp-i-want-to-shout-from-the-rooftops/s/12148.
Sister Michelle D. Craig, Young Women general presidency counselor, 2018-23, "Eyes To See," October 2020 general conference.

MADRE

Julie Ann Lake-Díaz

DIVINE NATURE AND DESTINY

SERVE. BE LOVE.
Trina Caudle

> I have inherited divine qualities, which I will strive to develop. — Young Women Personal Progress, value of Divine Nature

The most sincere prayer of my heart — ever — has been to know how to teach my children to be like Jesus. As a new mom, I read all the Church materials about parenting that I could get my hands on, and took it to the Lord. How do I teach my children to become like the Savior? The clear-as-day answer from the Spirit was a single word: SERVE.

As my kids grew, we worked on being kind to each other. I organized "family service projects" to bake treats for our ministering families, buy toys for toy drives, and fill backpacks with school supplies for children in foster care. We did great for a while and then got busy with our own things, so service faded as a priority. I asked again. The answer was again crystal clear and the same: SERVE.

> **The most sincere prayer of my heart — ever — has been to know how to teach my children to be like Jesus.**

We cycled through this for years — I prayed, got the answer of SERVE, I created goals and projects for my family, we did them until we slid into indifference, I prayed and asked the same question ... After a few years of this, the answer grew substantially more stern and very annoyed. The final answer was, "I already told you. SERVE." I have never prayed about that question again. I know the answer and it's not going to change.

As a Latter-day Saint in the Young Women program — both as a youth and an adult leader — I participated in the Personal Progress program and recited the Values frequently: faith, divine nature, individual worth, knowledge, choice and accountability, good works, integrity, and virtue. They are, as I'm sure President Ardeth G. Kapp hoped, embedded into my soul and part of how I move through this world. I wasn't surprised to receive the prompting to teach my children to serve, because I've always participated in a lot of service. The goals and projects of Good Works in Personal Progress were easy to complete because they were tangible assignments: bake the cookies, babysit the neighbor's toddler, rake the leaves, organize the library books, sing Christmas carols at the senior center ...

DIVINE NATURE AND DESTINY

The scripture we studied for Divine Nature had its own list of attributes: "That by these ye might be partakers of the divine nature ... giving all diligence, add to your faith virtue; and to virtue knowledge; and to knowledge temperance; and to temperance patience; and to patience godliness; and to godliness brotherly kindness; and to brotherly kindness charity. For if these things be in you, they make you that ye shall neither be barren nor unfruitful in the knowledge of our Lord Jesus Christ." (2 Peter 1:4-8)

It caught my attention that the attributes listed in that order build on each other and culminate in developing charity, the pure love of Christ.

> Charity is the pure love of Christ, and it endureth forever; and whoso is found possessed of it at the last day, it shall be well with him. Wherefore, pray unto the Father with all the energy of heart, that ye may be filled with this love, which he hath bestowed upon all who are true followers of his Son, Jesus Christ; that ye may become the [children] of God; that when he shall appear we shall be like him, for we shall see him as he is; that we may have this hope; that we may be purified even as he is pure. — Moroni 7:47-8

I am grateful, and very relieved, that we don't have to generate Christlike love from our own hearts by sheer force of will — we can pray and ask for it and it will be given to us! I envision a giant ceramic pitcher over my head, with love pouring out over me in the great waves of a full waterfall, and when I have a particularly irritating person in mind while pondering this, I actually do start to feel better about them.

Sister Mary Ellen Edmunds, Director of Training at the Missionary Training Center in Provo when I attended there, taught simply and clearly that love is a verb, and that's where my prompting of SERVE lands.

> **I am grateful, and very relieved, that we don't have to generate Christlike love from our own hearts by sheer force of will — we can pray and ask for it and it will be given to us!**

Love without service, like faith without works, is dead. You can serve without love, I suppose, but I don't think you can have genuine love without serving—you cannot feel compassion without feeling compelled to help in some way, to do what you can. Love is thus a powerful, peaceful force for good. [1]

The secret is in progression — to grow from DOING like Jesus to BEING like Jesus. Do the service to develop Christlike love for others, because "God is love." (1 John 4:16)

I was in a Relief Society discussion about charity and service, and a woman complained that she was spread too thin — she had to love God, and love her neighbor, and love herself, and do all the service while she maintained a job and raised her children, and it was all a hot mess. That's what she called love and service: "a hot mess." It got my attention as strange because this woman is a genuinely kind person who had not previously given any impression or hint that she felt service was a chore. I thought that day, "What if we just love? What if we stop putting life into a checklist and just BE LOVE?" Only love.

One year around Easter, I decided my scripture study would focus on charity. I started with the Topical Guide and looked up every verse about charity and love, and a pattern very clearly stood out: it doesn't matter what we do, or when, or how, if we don't care about the people around us. The scriptures are explicit that charity is the core of all divine qualities and without it, all other attributes are just going through the motions. "Wherefore, the Lord God hath given a commandment that all men should have charity, which charity is love. And except they should have charity they were nothing." (2 Nephi 26:30, also 1 Corinthians 13:1-3, Moroni 7:44) Alma 34 goes even further. After a long list of situations for prayer and fasting, "Do not suppose this is all; for after ye have done all these things, if ye turn away the needy, and the naked, and visit not the sick and afflicted, and impart of your substance, if we have, to those who stand in need — I say unto you, if ye do not any of these things, behold your prayer is vain and availeth you nothing, and ye are as hypocrites who do deny the faith. Therefore, if you do not remember to be charitable, ye are as dross, which the refiners do cast out, (it being of no worth) and is trodden under foot of men." (Alma 34:28-9)

> **The Divine Nature of our Heavenly Parents and the Savior is LOVE.**

All of these puzzle piece experiences are independent snapshots through my life, but they come together to form a larger picture: I firmly believe that the Divine Nature of our Heavenly Parents and the Savior is LOVE. I believe that with the same level of conviction that I believe the Book of Mormon is the word of God and that families are eternal. This is one of my core tenets.

Divine nature is not just about Personal Progress and girls from the 1980s and 90s. Developing charity — our actual, literal divine nature — and becoming Christlike is for all people, regardless of gender, ethnicity, or any other category of humans. And how do we develop our divine nature and become like Jesus Christ ... "I already told you. SERVE."

The bonus is that becoming like Christ isn't even the end. The ultimate goal is to return to our Heavenly Parents and be like THEM.

> At the end of this process [of life], our Heavenly Parents will have sons and daughters who are their peers, their friends, and their colleagues. We also will be gods. We will be able to love perfectly, like Them. We will be able to choose right freely, like Them. We will prize and cherish and never infringe on the agency of others, like Them. In other words, we will be able to be trusted with the powers of a god because we have acquired the perfect love and self-control and attributes of a god. — Sister Chieko Okazaki

We must SERVE, we must DO love, and we must BECOME love. Our Divine Nature of LOVE is the key to all the happy endings in every movie and book, and it is the key to the happy ending of our lives and eternity.

SOURCES

Mary Ellen Edmunds, Relief Society General Board member, 1986-97, Love is a Verb (Salt Lake City: Deseret Book, 1995), p. 1.
Chieko Okazaki, Sanctuary, (Salt Lake City: Deseret Book, 1997), 81.

STUDY HELPS
Divine Nature and Destiny

"Mother in Heaven" Gospel Topics essay footnote

Footnote 8: "The Family: A Proclamation to the World," September 1995. By the First Presidency (President Gordon B. Hinckley).

Study 1

> "Divine: (adj) of the nature of proceeding from or pertaining to God; sacred; heavenly; excellent. Divinity: (n) the character of being godly or divine; God. Nature: (n) the essential characteristic of a person or a thing." – Webster's Handy College Dictionary (1972)

> "Divine: (adj) relating to or being God or a God; supremely god; superb; heavenly. Nature: (n) the inherent quality of constitution of a person or thing; one's natural instincts or way of life." – The Merriam-Webster Dictionary (2022)

Using these definitions, list the characteristics you feel best describe the divine nature of Heavenly Mother.

Why did you choose these characteristics? What makes them heavenly characteristics?

As women and men, what do we need to do to develop these characteristics in life? Think outside the box.

Study 2

> Sisters, I testify that when you stand in front of your Heavenly Parents and you look into [Heavenly Mother's] eyes and behold Her countenance, any questions you ever had about the role of women in the kingdom will evaporate into the rich celestial air because at that moment you will see standing directly in front of you your divine nature and destiny. – Bishop Glen L. Pace [1]

Have you ever had questions about the role of women in the Church? How does understanding Heavenly Mother help alleviate some concerns? How might it increase cognitive dissonance? What can you do within your sphere of influence to elevate the role of women?

DIVINE NATURE AND DESTINY

Regardless of being male or female, what do you envision your first meeting with Heavenly Mother to be like?

Study 3

> This is a family centered Church in doctrine and practice. Our understanding of the nature and purpose of God the Eternal Father explains our destiny and our relationship in his eternal family. Our theology begins with the Heavenly Parents. Our highest aspiration is to be like Them. ...The fulness of eternal salvation is a family matter. – Elder Dallin H. Oaks [2]

Find stories, biographies or other accounts of your direct ancestors. As you read about their lives, make a list of experiences and trials they went through to become eternal families. How were they examples of a family-centered church?

If you are a journal keeper, go back to entries that you may have about when you became an eternal family in the temple. In place of a journal entry write down your memories of the time you and your family became an eternal family. This might include shared memories with your spouse.

What does "home-centered, church-supported" mean to you? How does this impact your parenting?

What can you do to encourage equal partnership in your family? What can you do to elevate the role of women within your family?

Study 4

> Born of a noble birthright, God is your father. He loves you. He and your Mother in Heaven value you beyond measure. ... You are unique, one of a kind, made of the eternal intelligence which gives you claim to eternal life. ... The whole intent of the gospel plan is to provide opportunity for each of you to reach your fullest potential, which is eternal progression and the possibility of godhood." – President Spencer W. Kimball [3]

Think of ways you are unique, one of a kind, that give you a claim to eternal life? How can you continue to develop these traits leading to eternal life?

In what way has your understanding of your divine nature and destiny grown or developed while studying this section?

DIVINE NATURE AND DESTINY

What choices should you make now to reach your divine destiny in the next life?

Study 5

Ponder the blessings for women named by President Russell M. Nelson: [4]

- Increased spiritual discernment and the ability to find joy in offering relief to others.
- Wisdom to discern what is needful and not run faster than they are able.
- Courage to live up to divine privilege as covenant daughters of God.
- Realize that their divine gifts as daughters of God give them power not only to change lives but to change the world.

What are some things we can do to develop these qualities?

What have you discovered about your own divine privilege?

What has the Spirit already helped you discern regarding what is needful in your life and/or family?

Is there a specific change you're waiting to muster up the courage to tackle?

Suggested Reading

"Your Purpose," Becky Edwards, *Cherish* book 1, p.207
"No Plan Without Her," Lisa Crawford, *Cherish* book 2, p.254

1 Glen L. Pace, "The Divine Nature and Destiny of Women," BYU Devotional, Provo, UT, March 9, 2010.
2 Dallin H. Oaks, "Apostasy and Restoration," April 1995 general conference.
3 Spencer W. Kimball, "Privileges and Responsibilities of Sisters", first General Women's Conference, October 1978.
4 Mary Richards, "Power of covenant-keeping women celebrated during Relief Society anniversary worldwide gathering," Church News, March 17, 2024,
thechurchnews.com/leaders/2024/03/17/worldwide-relief-society-anniversary-devotional-president-nelson-covenants-priesthood-power/.

7. DESIGNERS OF THE DIVINE PLAN

"'We are part of a **divine plan designed by Heavenly Parents** who love us,' taught Elder M. Russell Ballard of the Quorum of the Twelve Apostles."

Mother in Heaven essay, paragraph 4

THE SAVIOR HAS ALWAYS BEEN THE PLAN

The Church of Jesus Christ of Latter-day Saints refers to our soul's progression through the spirit world, birth and life on the earth, our death, resurrection, and eternal life, all through Jesus Christ, as the plan of salvation or the plan of happiness. In our doctrine, this great plan of happiness was presented to us and accepted by us in the council in heaven. It is glorious. It is a love story of learning, trial, overcoming, redemption, progression and exaltation. It is the greatest love story ever told – "For God so loved the world that He gave His Only Begotten Son, that whosoever believeth in Him should not perish, but have everlasting life." (John 3:16)

Christ's Atonement is the plan for our own individual progression and work to do, developing our agency into spiritual sovereignty, and reuniting with our Heavenly Parents in eternity.

The Topical Guide entry, "Plan of Salvation" opens with these words: "Before we were born on the earth, we lived with our Heavenly Parents as Their spirit children." We immediately come to the knowledge of our Heavenly Mother and Her presence in our premortal life.

An Apostle of the Lord declared that Heavenly Mother's involvement in designing this divine plan is our doctrine. In April 2022 general conference, Elder Renlund said, "The doctrine of a Heavenly Mother comes by revelation and is a distinctive belief among Latter-day Saints … What we do know is summarized in a gospel topic found in our Gospel Library."

What IS revealed about our Mother in Heaven's involvement in designing the divine plan is within the essay, directly quoting Elder M. Russell Ballard: "We are part of a divine plan designed by Heavenly Parents who love us." How does the knowledge that She also designed the plan change our thinking and perceptions? How can this knowledge change our language to be more doctrinally accurate?

"Your [Father and] Mother in Heaven value you beyond any measure. You are unique, one of a kind, made of the eternal intelligence which gives you claim upon eternal life. Let there be no question in your mind about your value as an individual. The whole intent of the gospel plan is to provide an opportunity for each of you to reach your fullest potential, which is eternal progression and the possibility of godhood." – President Spencer W. Kimball

Dale G. Renlund, "Your Divine Nature and Eternal Destiny," April 2022 general conference.
M. Russell Ballard, When Thou Art Converted: Continuing Our Search for Happiness (Salt Lake City: Deseret Book, 2001), 62.
Spencer W. Kimball, "Privileges and Responsibilities of Sisters," October 1978 general conference.

DESIGNERS OF THE DIVINE PLAN

FROM MY MOTHER

Amber Eldredge

TENDER

Amber Eldredge

DESIGNERS OF THE DIVINE PLAN

WE ARE GOOD BECAUSE SHE IS GOOD
Ashli Carnicelli

"We are part of a divine plan designed by Heavenly Parents who love us." [1]

In our premortal life, we lived with our Heavenly Parents as Their spirit children. (D&C 138:55-6) We were present at the heavenly council in which Heavenly Father presented the divine plan of salvation, also known as "the great plan of happiness" for us. (Alma 42:5, 8) The elements of this plan include a physical body subject to pain, temptation, affliction, sin and death (Moses 6:48); opposition in all things (2 Nephi 2:11); agency (Helaman 14:30); divinely appointed ordinances and laws of the gospel necessary for us to gain our eternal life (D&C 6:13); and an Atonement (Helaman 5:11) made for our sins and transgressions against the laws and ordinances by the use of our agency. This eternal life includes allowing us to become joint heirs with Jesus Christ. (Romans 8:16-17)

"And the way is prepared from the fall of man, and salvation is free." [2]

In the council in heaven, Jesus Christ was chosen to be the Messiah and provide the Atonement on our behalf. Through His Atonement, we can repent of our sins and be changed. We can do this as many times as it takes to change. As we change, we grow up unto the Lord (Helaman 3:21) and become perfect or whole through Him. (Moroni 10:32) The fruit of this change of heart and of eternal life is a fulness of joy. The entire purpose of this divine plan is for every one of us to have a fulness of joy. [3]

> **While the details of our Heavenly Mother's involvement in the design of the plan have not yet been revealed, the existence of a pathway of progression through the Savior to gain eternal life and a fulness of joy reveals MUCH about Her to me.**

While the details of our Heavenly Mother's involvement in the design of the plan have not yet been revealed, the existence of a pathway of progression through the Savior to gain eternal life and a fulness of joy reveals MUCH about Her to me.

First, the scriptures tell us that we were created in the image of God. In both Moses 2:26 and Genesis 1:26, we read: "And I, God, created man in mine own image, in the image of mine Only Begotten created I him; male and female created I them."

And here is where it gets SO good — the book of Abraham gives further light and knowledge: "And the Gods took counsel among themselves and said: Let us go down and form man in our image, after our likeness; So the Gods went down to organize man in their own image, in the image of the Gods to form they him, male and female to form they them." (Abraham 4:26-27)

After each day of creation in which each element of the world was organized, it was pronounced good by God. After man was created in the image of God, God said, "all things which I had made were good." (Moses 2:31, Genesis 1:31) As we know and understand that WE are good, we can also know and understand that SHE is good, as we were created in Her image.

When I was eleven months old, my twenty-year-old birth mother gave me up for adoption. My parents who adopted me are loving and wonderful, yet I felt a longing and a loss and a lost sense of identity. As I grew physically, I had no model to look to. Would I be tall? Would I be short? What kind of body would I develop when I became a woman? Why did I have a bump on my nose? Why was my talent singing and why was I so terrible at math? What nationalities did I have in my heritage? Who would I grow up to become? I had more questions than answers as a child, and then as a teenager. I could not fully know who I was until I fully knew who I came from! The longing to find my biological mother was an inescapable ache — both an instinct and a profound need. The instinct to connect with the source of my being. The need to return to the arms of my first earthly bond, the mother, the center of my universe as an infant.

> **As a convert to the Church of Jesus Christ of Latter-day Saints, I understand the soul's yearning for our Mother in Heaven, to find a deep sense of identity, and to be declared "good" from a spiritual perspective.**

I believe it is the same as we are spirit children of our Heavenly Parents, especially for women. I understand this yearning from the earthly perspective. As a convert to the Church of Jesus Christ of Latter-day Saints, I understand the soul's yearning for our Mother in Heaven, to find a deep sense of identity, and to be declared "good" from a spiritual perspective.

So many things in the world may make us question our own value and our own nature. We may have questions arise such as "Am I good?" "Am I enough?" "Am I valuable?" or "Am I worthwhile?" The divine plan answers a resounding YES to all of these questions in our hearts! The divine plan answers who we are and whose we are, and it is good! SO good!

The Lord has blessed my husband and me to become the parents of four daughters. Becoming a mother myself felt terrifying and triggering and anxiety producing – I'm sure much as entering into mortality felt, although I don't remember. Becoming a mother myself gave me a new perspective as an adoptee. My biological mother gave me up for adoption to my parents because she wanted me to have opportunities and experiences that she could not provide with me at her side. I think of our Heavenly Mother saying goodbye to us in the spirit world before coming to earth, knowing that mortality would provide all that She knows that we need, even though the separation is painful for both parties in the short term. I think about Her pain at giving Her Only Begotten Son to atone for us and grant us our eternal salvation.

My greatest wish for my daughters is their joy. As their mom, there is nothing I want more for them than to have all that they need. From a temporal perspective, that includes clothing and shelter and food and loving care. From a spiritual perspective, it is learning the gospel, the opportunity to progress, a relationship with Jesus Christ, salvation, eternal life, and to receive exaltation defined as "a feeling or state of extreme happiness." My birth mother wanting me to have a happy life in which all my needs were met was a reflection of her great love for me. My wanting these things for my children is a reflection of my great love for them. The divine plan of happiness is a reflection of our Mother in Heaven's great love for us!

There isn't anything I wouldn't sacrifice for my daughters and their well being. I have sacrificed sleep, my physical body, time, resources, and opportunities to ensure that my daughters are provided for. This brings to mind our Heavenly Father and our Heavenly Mother sending their Only Begotten Son, their perfect Lamb, to the earth to atone for us. That sacrifice is so immense it is unfathomable to me! But it tells me two things—first, that our Heavenly Mother is GOOD and full of love for us, and second, that we are incredibly precious and of infinite worth to Her and our Heavenly Father. They and Jesus Christ gave all, that we may fulfill Their divine and loving plan for us.

SOURCES

1 M. Russell Ballard, When Thou Art Converted: Continuing Our Search for Happiness (Salt Lake City: Deseret Book, 2001), 62.
2 2 Nephi 2:4
3 2 Nephi 2:25; Gospel Topics "Council in Heaven," churchofjesuschrist.org/study/manual/gospel-topics

STUDY HELPS
Designers of the Divine Plan

"Mother in Heaven" Gospel Topics essay footnote

Footnote 9: When Thou Art Converted: Continuing Our Search for Happiness, Deseret Book (2001), p. 62. By Elder M. Russell Ballard.

Study 1

> "Design(er): (n) the person who plans a detailed pattern; plan, contrives; or makes an original plan." —Webster's Handy College Dictionary (1972, p.130)

> "Designer: (n) One who does creative plans for a project or structure. Design: (v) to conceive or plan out in the mind; an underlying scheme that governs functioning, developing, and unfolding." —The Merriam-Webster Dictionary (2022, p.111)

Based on these definitions, how would you describe Heavenly Mother and Heavenly Father as designers? Why did you choose those descriptions?

What is the "divine plan?" How are you participating in this divine plan as a designer of your life?

How would you explain the phrase "designers of the divine plan" to someone who does not have the same knowledge or beliefs as you?

Study 2

> In his 1876 Semi-annual general conference address, Brigham Young included "eternal Mother and "eternal Daughters" who after the resurrection will "be prepared to frame earths like unto ours and like unto people them in the same manner as we have been brought forth by our [Heavenly] Parent's. [1]

> Elder Milton R. Hunter, Seventy, taught that the exaltation and endless lives that Celestial women and men share include "the power to create or organize mortal worlds. [2]

What does "the power to create or organize mortal worlds" mean to you?

DESIGNERS OF THE DIVINE PLAN

What are ways that we prepare ourselves in this life to fulfill this statement of being "prepared to frame earths" in the next life?

As co-creator with Heavenly Father of this world, what do you believe Heavenly Mother's responsibilities are? Explain why you choose those responsibilities.

If you were creating worlds as Elder Hunter talks about, how do you think the creation would be done?

What additional blessings do celestial men and women receive?

How do you exercise your own creative powers in your life?

Study 3

> In addition to her participation in creation, Heavenly Mother helps Heavenly Father in the Plan of Salvation. Elder M. Russell Ballard taught that we are part of a divine plan, designed by Heavenly Parents who love us. [3]

How would you explain the Plan of Salvation to someone unfamiliar with this plan?

Using your explanation, make a visual aide to show the plan of salvation. Identify the parts of the plan you feel Heavenly Mother could have been involved in developing.

"Elder Jeffery Holland and his wife Patricia taught that our Mother and our Father are involved in the ongoing process of creating everything around us and are "doing so lovingly and carefully and masterfully.'" [4] Why are Heavenly Mother and Heavenly Father's jobs not done when Their children leave the preexistence?

Suggested Reading

"Weaver," Kayla Gissman, *Cherish* book 1, p. 262.
"Mother Editor," Jessica Vergara, *Cherish* book 2, p. 299.

1. Paulsen, "A Mother There," 13.
2. Paulsen, "A Mother There," 14.
3. Paulsen, "A Mother There," 14.
4. Paulsen, "A Mother There," 15.

8. INFLUENCES FROM BEYOND

"President Harold B. Lee stated, 'We forget that we have a Heavenly Father and a Heavenly Mother who are even more concerned, probably, than our earthly father and mother, and that **influences from beyond** are constantly working to try to help us when we do all we can.'"

Mother in Heaven essay, paragraph 4

INVOLVED PARENTS

There is no end of sentiment written about the love and influence of mothers, from poets to politicians to religious leaders across the world. We appreciate mothers! Heavenly Mother, as the ultimate Mother, is no different. Latter-day Saint leaders across the history of the Church validate that She loves and influences our lives. In the mouth of two or three (or five) witnesses ...

> Our Heavenly Parents' love and concern for us continues to this very moment. – Elder Ballard [1]

> President Harold B. Lee shared the story of a man who struggled with smoking and one day, opened a pack of cigarettes. As he was about to light one, he "heard a voice say as gently as any worried mother might caution a careless son, 'Oh Bill, give up your cigarettes!'" He never smoked again. [2]

> On a particularly difficult day, or sometimes a series of difficult days, what would this world's inhabitants pay to know that heavenly parents are reaching across those same streams and mountains and deserts, anxious to hold them close? – Elder Holland [3]

> You are a beloved son or daughter of our Heavenly Parents. Their hearts yearn over you in joy and love. They want to give you all the treasures of eternity, and They hope steadfastly that you will be the kind of person who will want the riches of eternity – in other words, that you will follow the pathway marked out for you by the Savior and live a life that is guided by the principle of love. – Sister Okazaki [4]

> We wonder if our Heavenly Mother and Father must not be worried and concerned over some of our antics. It must be quite an occasion in heaven when our Heavenly Mother bid us a loving farewell for the time being! Perhaps, like earthly mothers, She thinks, 'They are so young, and they might forget for a moment.' – Elder John Longden [5]

We all have dark days and life challenges but our Heavenly Parents are more involved in our lives than we realize. How does this truth change those moments? How do you feel supported by Divine Parental love during difficult times?

M. Russell Ballard, Our Search for Happiness, (Salt Lake City: Deseret Book, 1993), 70.
Harold B. Lee, "The Influence and Responsibility of Women," Relief Society Magazine, Feb. 1964: 85.
Jeffrey R. Holland, "Belonging: A View of Membership," Ensign, April 1980.
Chieko Okazaki, Sanctuary, (Salt Lake City: Deseret Book, 1997), 97-8.
John Longden, "The Worth of Souls," Relief Society Magazine 44 (August 1957): 492-494.

INFLUENCES FROM BEYOND

GENERATIONS OF MOTHERS

Katie Garner

ACCESSING THE WISDOM OF THE DIVINE FEMININE

Jody Moore

I took my firstborn child to college in 2024 and I haven't been the same since. I knew it would be hard seeing him fly the nest. Especially since he's going somewhat reluctantly and with some fear and sadness of his own. But I didn't expect it to linger in my heart the way it has. It's hard to put my finger on what this feels like because it's not a death or tragedy. It's not even a bad thing. It's a very good and natural and healthy thing that has happened. It's just that I can't shake the feeling in my home that something is missing. Because something, or someone rather, IS missing. And it's my child.

This experience has caused me to reflect a good deal on my own mother and to feel more compassion for what her experience must have been like as she watched her five children leave home one after another. Intellectually, I understood that would be hard but now I am beginning to know it on an emotional level.

But equally powerful throughout this experience is how much I've considered my Heavenly Mother. What is She like? What does She know that I don't yet or couldn't possibly? How does She carry the burden of nurturing the entire human race? What must She be made of? And most importantly, how and when and where is Her influence found? How do we recognize it, call upon it, or channel it when needed? The truth is I don't know. To say anything otherwise would be a stretch at best. I don't know how She operates or how we best hear Her. I only know that I sometimes have a moment of wisdom and clarity that couldn't possibly be my own. It's less like a figuring-out and more like a remembering of something I knew before. It's divine and feminine and it's the closest I get to feeling Her guide me from beyond.

> *It's less like a figuring-out and more like a remembering of something I knew before.*

And here's the best part.

When I want to connect with my earthly mother, I don't wait for her to call. I pick up the phone and see if she's available. And I do the same with my Mother in Heaven. But instead of a phone, I grab a notebook and a pen. I ask myself a really good question and then I let the answer come. I use the page to ask and then I use the page to receive the answer. I don't try and effort myself to knowing the answer. I just feel my way to the answer that feels true in that moment. It isn't always pretty

INFLUENCES FROM BEYOND

or cohesive, but it's the closest I've come to Her divine guidance from beyond.

Recently I asked Her this question about the transitional part of life I find myself in as my children grow older and need me less:

Dear Feminine Divine,
What would you have me know about my life's purpose right now?

And here was Her reply:

Dear Jody,

It's sweet that you think your life is always meant for something big. Something noble. Something generous and moving and challenging. The truth is that you are right. And also, you are wrong.

Your life is meant for all the experiences a woman can have. For pleasure and joy and fun as well as heartache and struggle and fear. You're meant to try it all like a buffet of possibility and expansiveness. All of it molding you into new versions of yourself that will only be satisfied momentarily and then curious about what's next. You're right about this part. It's delicious to be alive.

But you are wrong when you believe any of it can be pinned down and put into a box. Even with beautiful wrapping and a giant bow, the box can never hold the complexity of a woman in a human body having the experience of being alive. It can never be pinned down in the way you believe it can. Not even for a second. It's constantly changing, constantly evolving, and ever messy until the end of this human life.

> **Your life is meant for all the experiences a woman can have. For pleasure and joy and fun as well as heartache and struggle and fear.**

When you were a young girl, you used to wear an apron and imagine what it would be like to have children to bake cookies for and a home to curate to your liking. Do you remember this? You thought that being a mother would give your life a bigger purpose than the exhausting pursuit of college credits and jobs that barely paid the bills. You knew that being a mother was bigger than your concerns over what to wear and whether your hair was cooperating today, and you were right but also give an answer to you today. The real answer is: nothing.

INFLUENCES FROM BEYOND

wrong. The classes and the jobs and the clothes and the hair ... that part is good too. That was you finding yourself, embracing yourself, and expressing yourself and it's all good. And being a mother is simply another part. Not better. Not more of anything or less of anything. Another experience. Just another opportunity to become.

But become what? That's the question you seem to be asking, and I'll attempt to give you an answer today. The real answer is nothing.

There is nothing for you to become. There is no purpose you need to justify your existence in this world. There is no goal to seek after that will validate your life. There is no going or doing or getting or having that will ever give you what you really seek because what you seek is not available in this life. What you seek is to finish. To check all the boxes and cross the items off the list. But there is no finishing because there is no finish line. There is only more and more and more. More boxes. More races. More items on the list to be done. But do not fear. This is not the bad news you may think it is in this moment. Let me explain.

> **There is no purpose you need to justify your existence in this world.**

Remember when you were 21 years old and you decided to run a marathon? Your friend Jen was a marathon runner and you looked up to her like a big sister. She noticed you took up running to stay fit in college and suggested you go for it. You thought she was crazy. Maybe she was. But you signed up anyway. And then you ran and ran and ran more than you knew your legs could go. You got blisters so big the doctor had to intervene. You developed knee problems you shouldn't have had at such a young age, and you wondered if you'd be able to finish when the big day came.

And then it came. Your whole family and some good friends came to cheer you on and support you and it was an experience still etched on your heart to this day. You can still see the sun coming up over the mountains as you hit mile 9. You can see the faces of the kids in the small towns who hoped you'd take their cup of water so they could feel they were making an important contribution to this event. You can hear the woman's voice at mile 25 when you thought you couldn't go one step further. She didn't know your name but wanted you to know she saw you, so she looked at the numbers on your race bib and called out, "Go 6573! You can do it! Don't quit!" You decided to believe her even though you knew she had no idea if you could really do it.

But you did.

INFLUENCES FROM BEYOND

You crossed the finish line, and you felt the joy and sting and relief of finishing something you'd put in so much time working toward. Your parents and friends were so proud of you. And you. You were proud of you. For a moment you didn't wish you were better or different. You just saw how amazing it feels to work toward something hard and want to give up but to override that part of you and finish strong.

And you've been chasing that feeling ever since.

But that feeling is only powerful because it comes infrequently and in different ways and intensities. But you've felt it a lot. When your babies were born. When you got married. When you moved back to Southern California where you left a piece of your heart years ago. When you speak on a stage you almost always feel it. Sometimes it shows up after a great coaching call where you know you just changed someone's heart in a significant way. When your mom has a good day, and her pain and struggle seem to be getting better. It comes here and there but it's not the norm.

It's not supposed to be.

It's not a feeling that likes to be chased. It is just the natural climax of living your life in alignment with peace and love and focus and commitment. When you go after something big and you have fun doing it, you often end up with this feeling.

> So your life's purpose, my love, is to live big in any way your heart feels called to do.

But the feeling isn't meant to last.

You're meant to come back down from the high and wonder what's next. That's the way of this human life. Over and over again until you die. Don't think of it as dissatisfied. Think of it as the natural ebb and flow of the tides of the ocean. There is a peaceful, beautiful, natural rhythm to it if you allow it to be and don't fight it.

But don't forget about the sun coming up behind the mountains at mile 9 and the small children handing out water, and the stranger cheering you on through your pain. Not to mention the training and learning and strengthening you did to prepare. That is the journey toward the destination and that is the real purpose of this life. Your purpose and everyone else's at the same time. It's not unique or mysterious. It's just living a full life.

So your life's purpose, my love, is to live big in any way your heart feels called to do. Find impossible problems and throw arrows of love at them. Show up in big ways wherever you feel curious or drawn, but show up in small ways in your town, your neighborhood, or your home as well. Be light. Be laughter. Be joy. Let the heavy stuff go.

INFLUENCES FROM BEYOND

You've never once been right about what challenges lie ahead. They are always surprises you didn't see coming. So, you can stop trying to predict them and just relax into the joy of the moment. Worry is not preventative after all. You don't have a purpose other than this. Which doesn't mean to surrender to mediocrity. It means go big. Risk it all. Go all in on anything you feel curious about. Having nothing to prove means there is nothing to lose. Just enjoy it all. You're right on track.

- *Mother Divine*

And there you have it. This is what She told me when I asked her my question. This is the wisdom that lives within me in the feminine divine I inherited from Her. It's the honest truth that I know but forget. It's the reality of our humanity that gets lost in the doing and being and having. But if I stop for a moment and receive Her love, I find it again.

This is the wisdom that lives within me in the feminine divine I inherited from Her.

What questions do you have for Mother Divine? Perhaps She is waiting for you to ask.

STUDY HELPS
Influences From Beyond

"Mother in Heaven" Gospel Topics essay footnote

Footnote 10: "The Influence and Responsibility of Women," Relief Society Magazine, February 1964, p. 85. By Elder Harold B. Lee. (Word search for "General Session of the Relief Society Annual General Conference".)

Study 1

> "Influencer: power or control to affect others by authority, persuasion, example; a person or thing that exerts such power." — Webster's Handy College Dictionary (1972, p.243)

> "Influence: The act or power of producing an effect without apparent force or direct authority; the power or capacity of causing an effect in indirect or intangible ways; one that exerts influence." — The Merriam-Webster Dictionary (2022, p.377)

In the definitions for influence and influencer, which words describe Heavenly Mother and Heavenly Father's effect on us from beyond?

How have you been nurtured by the mother figures in your life? How have you been nurtured by the father figures in your life? How is their nurturing different? How is it similar?

How have you been nurtured by your Heavenly Father? Have you had experiences when you have been nurtured by your Heavenly Mother? How are they different? How are they similar?

Study 2

> But what about the eternal Father and Mother? Have they no claim upon us? Should we not return to them and resume relations of a power of love? Heavenly Mother and Father are not just Heavenly Parents-they are our Eternal Parents. They will guide our destinies forever. There is no end to other adventures we may have together. — Elder Orson F. Whitney [1]

INFLUENCES FROM BEYOND

Based on Elder Whitney's statement, what are some ways our Heavenly Parents can influence our lives?

What are some examples in the scriptures of our Heavenly Parents influencing someone's life?

When and how have you felt the influence of our Heavenly Parents?

Study 3

> Sometimes we think the whole job is up to us, forgetful that there are loved ones beyond our sight who are thinking about us and our children. We forget we have a Heavenly Father and a Heavenly Mother who are even more concerned, probably, than our Earthly father and mother, and that influences from beyond are constantly working to try to help us when we do all we can.
> — President Harold B. Lee [2]

How often have you felt the spirit of Heavenly Parents reaching out to you? Can you identify how you are reached? How do you cultivate that connection?

If you are a parent, how do you feel your love for your children compares with the omnipresent love of Heavenly Mother and Heavenly Father? Can you describe what makes the difference?

Suggested Reading

"Mothering through the Hard Elements with Heavenly Mother," Bethany Brady Spalding, *Cherish* book 1, p.303
"The Woman Whose Presence Lingers," Nathan Young, *Cherish* book 2, p.341

Orson F. Whitney, "We Walk by Faith," Improvement Era 19 (no. 5, May 1916), 7.
Harold B. Lee, "The Influence and Responsibility of Women."

9. CONNECTION

According to what is recorded in the Bible, Jesus Christ "taught His disciples to 'always pray unto the Father in my name'."

Mother in Heaven essay, paragraph 5

CONNECTION

A PERSONAL RELATIONSHIP

Prayer is vital in our tradition but there are many ways to feel our Mother's love, our Father's love, and the Savior's love. Prayer is only one touchpoint to Divinity.

We pray in the name of Jesus Christ, but we do not pray directly to Jesus Christ. We are still encouraged and expected to have a testimony of and relationship with the Savior. We are able to connect with Him even though we do not pray directly to Him.

> The Lord will show up and stand by you, and He will bless you where you are standing. He will meet you where you are, but He won't leave you there. He will bring you to a better place, a place of happiness and joy. — President Emily Belle Freeman

The same can be said and done with Heavenly Mother. Women have shared the variety of ways and times in which they feel close to Her: in childbirth, and in infertility. In mothering through food, and mothering through activities. Through the scriptures and through nature. Many have reported feeling Heavenly Mother show up for them in their lives, and have felt Her love and the joy of having this fulness of knowledge.

Because of this, many have felt inspired to shout their praises from the rooftops- through poetry, art and music. This joyous approbation is appropriate and is welcomed by God! "For ye shall go out with joy, and be led forth with peace: the mountains and the hills shall break forth into singing, and all the trees of the field shall clap their hands." (Isaiah 55:12)

Because we are all unique, no one should ever say, "Everyone will connect with Heavenly Father and Mother like this." Consider what makes you YOU — what makes you feel complete, what brings you joy, what energizes you. Focus there to connect with our Heavenly Mother and Father in that moment. If God is infinite, there are infinite touchpoints to reach Them. How can you connect to God?

Mary Richards, "President Freeman and Sister Dennis testify of Jesus Christ through West Africa ministry," The Church News, November 22, 2023. Thechurchnews.com. Emily Belle Freeman, Young Women general president, Young Single Adult Devotional, Egbeda Ward, Lagos, Nigeria , November 12, 2023.

TO BE KNOWN AND SEEN

Sarah Sabey

> That I may bring to pass my strange act, that I may pour out my Spirit upon all flesh. — D&C 95:4

When I was nine years old, God spoke to me. My parents were out of town and had left my younger sister and me with Sister Hathaway — a family friend — for the week. Most likely exhausted from our exuberance at our new environment, our caretaker invited us to go play at the park for an hour or two. She described the route there and told us that when we were ready to come home, we just needed to look for the house with the green pots.

We successfully made our way to the park where we played happily until near dinnertime, and that's when our troubles began. We walked all the way down the neighborhood street I could have sworn we had come from, but we never saw any green pots. We tried the next street over, and the next one. No pots, no Sister Hathaway. By now, it was beginning to get dark and cold. Having been raised by goodly LDS parents, my sister and I decided it was time to start praying.

When I was nine years old, God spoke to me.

Immediately, I felt something. I can't explain it. A strange sense of direction that was absolutely not self-motivated. A gut instinct that neither came from my gut nor felt instinctual. I felt suddenly and strongly that my sister and I ought to go back to the park.

But it made no sense. While I was unsure where Sister Hathaway's house was, I was very sure I would not find it at the playground. Instead, I suggested we try one more street. We walked the full length of the street. Still no green pots. It was quite dark now. The commuters were arriving home from the office, and we saw families gathering around dining tables through the windows.

"Sarah," my sister said, "I think we need to go back to the park."

Feeling still that pulling exterior to my own will, I nodded. We turned. A flash of bright headlights blinded us. Sister Hathaway sprang from the driver's seat and hugged us tight. "I've been running all over the park looking for you," she exclaimed.

CONNECTION

I know how all this sounds. It's a little trite, cliché, and sentimental. But here's the thing I can't get over: God spoke to me, a plain, privileged, unremarkable, middle-class, white, American, nine-year-old schoolgirl. God spoke to me. I felt it. A cavernous echoing. A flash of light. An unexpected knock on the door of my soul. It was there. It was strange. I have never, ever forgotten it.

I am relatively new to the search for Heavenly Mother. For most of my life, the project felt almost inaccessible. Heavenly Father already feels so mysterious to me, and Heavenly Mother even more so. I am a firm believer in Augustine's proclamation: "We are speaking of God; what marvel, if you do not comprehend? For if you comprehend, it is not God." There's so little I know, and so much I do not comprehend. In my yearnings for God, I have frequently felt small, strange, but also — most astonishingly — seen.

For me, Heavenly Mother has been a similar revelation.

When Joseph saw God, it was not the God he imagined. It was not the expansion of his imagination into the world. It was strange. It was uncomfortable to have hidden things unhidden, and to see that they were not exactly what he had assumed.

For me, Heavenly Mother has been a similar revelation. Making hidden things unhidden has taken a sometimes-wavering, sincere, and effortful seeking. And I have felt her. It's hard to describe. Divinity always is, for me. It's like an untamed "something else" humming within me but originating from somewhere beyond me. It's like a pair of hands gently tugging on the filaments of me. It's like the moment the metaphysical brushes upon the incarnational. It's like a mother's lullaby sounding both intimately familiar and entirely new. She has been a strange presence in my life, but a presence.

In her strangeness, I have felt companionship. I have felt in the baffling, gawky way I have always experienced divinity that there is something there. A mother there. That I am known. That I — an unremarkable, plain, privileged, middle-class, white, American housewife — am seen.

And it is this Mother — holy, strange, seeing, knowing, loving — that I, in turn, strive to see and know.

HER HAND

Emily Carruth Fuller

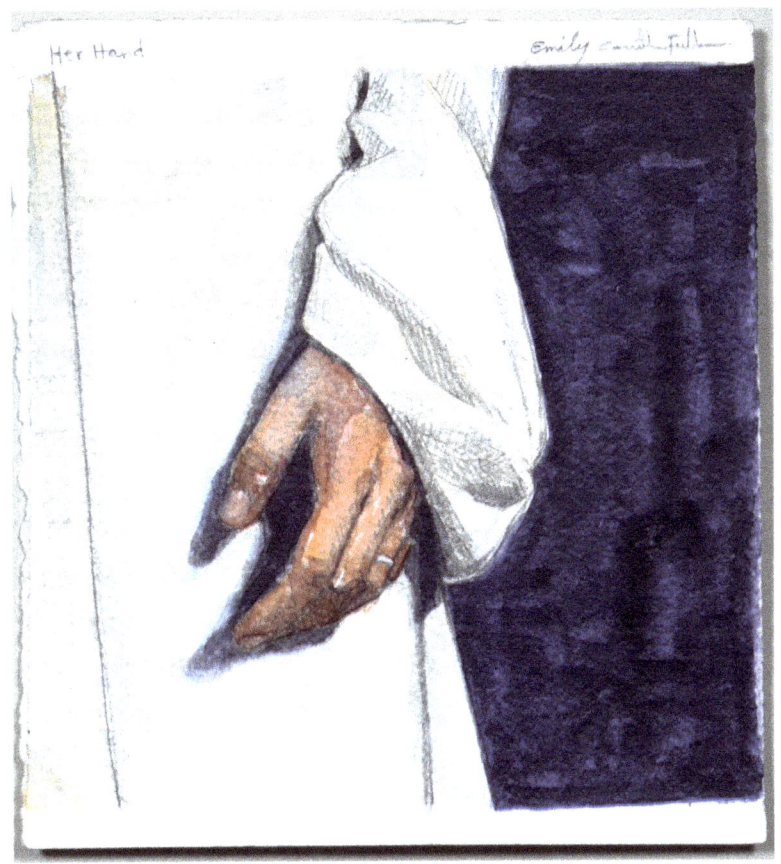

CONNECTION

WOMB
Thomas McConkie

What we call God matters.

I grew up learning to pray to "God the Father" as Jesus showed His apostles to do in the New Testament. There was a season in life where this name of God worked for me in an uncomplicated and straightforward way. God was my Heavenly Father and He loved me with all the tender love a parent naturally feels for His child. Though I couldn't appreciate it at the time, the name "Father" became the container that shaped my relationship to God, the way water takes the shape and hue of the vessel that contains it.

Not all people have the experience of wearing out one of God's names, but that's what happened to me. What had served as a beautiful container for me to deepen my relationship with God unexpectedly came to feel like a straitjacket. Maybe it was the painful relationship I had with my own father growing up that instigated my change in attitude. Maybe it was the cultural interpretation of "Father" along the Wasatch Front that felt to me like so many stuffy suits listening to dour organ music. Whatever it was, the reality of "God the Father" lost its magic for me.

For years after this "crisis of names" I refused to call on God at all. I didn't know there was an option other than "Father," and I was done with the stern disciplinarian always looking over me, brow knitted with disapproval, finger wagging imperiously. Then a meditation teacher handed me a classical text from the apocryphal sage known as the "Old Child." In this new language environment, the great "Tao" was said to be older than God Himself. The Tao is the "God" that gives birth to our idea of God, it suggested. This turn in language burst my budding adolescent mind into a fresh bloom of newfound devotion to the Sacred.

> **Not all people have the experience of wearing out one of God's names, but that's what happened to me.**

I lived in this name for many years, no longer relating to God as a person so much as a formless Presence that went beyond, yet still fully embraced all of form. From there, I naturally eased into a Buddhist worldview where the question of God was, more or less, set aside. It was the essence that I shared with the Buddha and all living beings, the nature of Nature, that was the Supreme Good. In realizing my Basic Nature, I came to feel an intimacy with everything that is.

In a quiet moment, many years into my life as a Buddhist practitioner, a Love too simple for words revealed itself to me in an instant, shattering everything I'd ever known, reminding me that I had always been Whole. Contrary to so much of my Buddhist training, I felt that this Love knew me and was calling me Home in a deeply personal way. What I later came to understand as the Love of Christ had been relentlessly pursuing me, the beloved, all along.

I let this new substance take root in my heart. I took on Christ's yoke and felt its ease. Meanwhile, the same prescient teacher who had introduced me to Taoism twenty years prior, the same teacher who always seemed to know exactly what name of God would be the very best food for my soul, that same teacher shared with me the 99 names of Allah.

The Sufi world is so vast, I hardly ever made it past the very first name: Ya Rahman.

The root of this name, "rahm", means "womb" in Arabic. It suggests that God's infinite, merciful Love envelops us as a womb. Just as an unborn child can receive all the warmth, all the rest, all the nourishment it will ever need to grow into fullness, the Womb suspends us in a medium of Divine Love that is not only our manna, but is also at once the substance of who we are.

It was all in the name. The symbolic number of 99 in Sufism suggests that the names of God are infinite, God's qualities are infinite. When we realize this, we realize we can call on God as we need God to appear to us. Worship and devotion in this attitude become "choose your own adventure." In our creative act of naming, God manifests as the very form that our heart cries out for.

> **The root of this name, "rahm", means "womb" in Arabic. It suggests that God's infinite, merciful Love envelops us as a womb.**

I had to ask the question at some point: Why didn't anyone teach me more of the Feminine aspect of the Divine? Why didn't Jesus say more about His Heavenly Mother to His disciples? (Or maybe He did?) Better yet, why don't we Christians practice resting knowingly in the Divine Womb of God's infinite Mercy?

Rather than getting caught in the theological tangle these worthy questions give rise to, I've come to an intuitive response in my own life.

CONNECTION

To rest in the Womb, to commune with the Feminine aspect of the Divine, I don't need to learn structured prayers or work out a rationale. Just as my mother held me as a child, wordlessly, her attention rapt as I gurgled and cooed and drank in her nourishing gaze, I soften right now and feel the Mother of all beings loving me into fullness. She does this whether I remember Her or not.

In the Womb of Divine Love, I am always, already known. I am heard before I can even speak the words. Every thought is already Her thought. Every name I could ever call Her, ever imagine, is just another quality that She generously gives birth to in Her worlds without number.

> **To rest in the Womb, to commune with the Feminine aspect of the Divine, I don't need to learn structured prayers or work out a rationale. Just as my mother held me as a child, wordlessly, her attention rapt as I gurgled and cooed and drank in her nourishing gaze, I soften right now and feel the Mother of all beings loving me into fullness. She does this whether I remember Her or not.**

STUDY HELPS
Connection

> Heavenly Mother
> Loves everyone dearly
> I feel Her spirit
> – Janice McArthur

"Mother in Heaven" Gospel Topics essay footnotes

Footnote 11: 3 Nephi 18:19-21; Matthew 6:6-9; John 17:1, 5, 21, 24-25; see also Matthew 4:10; Luke 4:8; and 3 Nephi 13:9; 17:15.

Footnote 12: President Gordon B. Hinckley, "Daughters of God," October 1991 general conference.

Study 1

"Connect: (v) to associate mentally; join; associate closely; establish communication or juncture. Connection: (n) the state of being connected; union; family relationships; distant relative; a bond to continuity." –Webster's Handy College Dictionary (1972, p.103)

"Connection: junction, union; logical relationship; family relationship; a mass of communication. –The Merriam-Webster Dictionary (2022, p.155-6)

What words from the definitions of connect and connection help define our relationship to Heavenly Mother? Why does that give meaning to you?

What are ways that you connect with the Savior, without praying directly to Him? How do you feel the Spirit?

Do you have a connection with Heavenly Mother? If so, how is that connection made? If not, what are some ways you can develop a connection with Her?

CONNECTION

Study 2

If you were to write a letter to Heavenly Mother, what would you tell Her? What do you feel is important for Her to know about you? Make a list of the ideas you would share with Heavenly Mother and the questions you would ask.

Using the list from question 1, write a letter to Heavenly Mother. What ways might you receive an answer to your letter?

Consider writing a journal entry about a time you have connected with Heavenly Mother. What did you learn from the connection? How did it make you feel?

How has your knowledge and testimony of the doctrine of Heavenly Mother grown? As Sister Holland advised, have you shared this knowledge with others?

Suggested Reading

"Acrostic," Trina Caudle, *Cherish* book 1, p. 325
"Letter to Mother", Megan Watson, *Cherish* book 1, p. 322-323
"Tending the Seeds of Life," Rebecca Young, *Cherish* book 2, p. 366-368

10. ETERNAL PROTOTYPE

"Indeed, as Elder Rudger Clawson wrote, 'We honor woman when we acknowledge Godhood in her **eternal Prototype**.'"

Mother in Heaven essay, paragraph 5

LOOK UP

Some people in the world are able to create something out of nothing. But most of us benefit from seeing a model of what's possible. The saying goes – if you can see it, you can be it.

We often refer to Christ as the Exemplar as we understand the value of having a model to emulate. "For I have given you an example, that ye should do as I have done to you." (John 13:15)

Artists, engineers, architects use prototypes to know what they're creating. Research shows the girls are more likely to go into STEM if they've seen a woman in STEM.

Who would we want our daughters to model? Our Mother in Heaven!

The same is true for all women. If we know and celebrate our Mother in Heaven, amazing reverberations happen! One, we can become like Her. Two, we understand our divine trajectory. And three, men and women both can understand more fully the divine order of partnership.

> Trees reach up for the light and grow in the process. So do we as sons and daughters of Heavenly Parents. Facing upward provides a loftier perspective than facing right or facing left. Looking up in search of holiness builds strength and dignity as disciples of Deity. – President Nelson

Paying attention to which direction we face and utilizing the Savior's Atonement has the potential to expand our souls in becoming like our Heavenly Parents... and to return home to Them.

Russell M. Nelson, "Thou Shalt Have No Other Gods Before Me," April 1996 general conference.

DIVINE DECONSTRUCTION

Carly White

BECOMING
McArthur Krishna

When I was in college, my horoscope told me that I would be a "ballerina, bull-doze driver, trapeze artist." I was a little bummed since I had planned on being a desert-princess-turned-bandit... with boots and a flowing cape.

> **This is the first reason it's vital to embrace Heavenly Mother as our eternal exemplar — Her existence shows us our trajectory.**

The thing is, the doctrine of our Heavenly Mother makes it clear we can become anything we want.

The Gospel Topics Essay definitively states that Heavenly Mother is our "eternal Prototype" for women — the archetypal model we pattern after. Prototypes can also be referred to as an original or the essential standard.

We need to know that our prototype for eternal progression is a designing, creating, loving, involved, influencing, co-equal partner God. (All doctrine from the Gospel Topics Essay!)

What are the benefits of knowing Heavenly Mother is the eternal prototype for women?

1- Eternal Prototype Means Soul Investment

This is the first reason it's vital to embrace Heavenly Mother as our eternal exemplar — Her existence shows us our trajectory. The women of the Church need a vision for their divine destiny. All of a sudden, women truly understand that their "destiny is godhood, not counselorhood." [1] In order to get to godhood, our souls need development. She is infinite — and so are our souls.

Yet there is a gap between the development of the soul we have now and a beautifully godly soul. (I'll speak for myself.)

Bridging that gap requires investment. There are many, many ways to invest in soul development. For some it may require resources to go back to school. For another it may just mean her family handles Thursday night needs so she has an evening to paint or read or even take a nap! For another it may mean carving out time to develop a talent. One thing is clear — growth requires an investment of some kind. If we want to model for our children that a woman's soul is worth investing in — that females become gods like our Mother — then we need to start now. I know we often think we don't have time or money, but give the gift of an eternal model to your family ... however that looks for you.

Elder Uchtdorf said, "Remember that you are of the royal house of the kingdom of God, daughters of Heavenly Parents, who reign throughout the universe. You have the spiritual DNA of God. You have unique gifts that originated in your spiritual creation and that were developed during the vast span of your premortal life." [2]

It's time to invest in growing those gifts!

And some of that soul investment may require excavation work. We may have old ideas about ourselves and our divine destiny that we need to clear out to enable growth. We may have inherited some models and habits that need tearing down. We certainly need to make space. As artist Carly White so luminously illustrates, that process may require some jackhammering.

> **Heavenly Mother is an example of the ultimate form of agency as a sovereign being.**

As our prototype, Heavenly Mother provides women with a clear vision of their divine destiny. Once women learn about "the eternal Prototype," and invest in growing ... our souls light up!

Let's get to it.

2- Eternal Prototype Means We Must Become Sovereign Women

Heavenly Mother is an example of the ultimate form of agency as a sovereign being. When a being has chosen over and over to rise to their best self... they eventually become a god. And we are embryonic gods! Since we know that Heavenly Mother is our eternal ideal... and we will become as She is... it follows that we also must become absolute rock stars at exercising our agency. Top notch professionals. Experts extraordinaire. (Because, really, the other no-agency option was not Jesus' plan, hear what I'm saying?). What does it mean for us to practice being sovereign beings? It means aligning with God, seeking personal revelation, and trusting that revelation— NO MATTER WHAT.

ETERNAL PROTOTYPE

That's easy to write and can be tough to live. And, that's ok. As Teryl Givens has taught— one of the first challenges of Eve and Adam's earth life experience was cognitive dissonance... or, the pains of learning to be sovereign. [3]

Until recently, we taught that women have a mediated relationship to God. This has changed in our temple worship ... but has it changed in our default settings? Has this changed in our marriages? In our decision-making? In our church councils?

This may seem like an obvious thing — but there are numerous ways being un-sovereign creeps in. For example, when a woman prays about accepting a new calling and feels strong personal revelation that she should refuse — does she share that insight and decline the calling? Even though we've been trained to never say no? When a wife and husband are praying about whether to take a job or buy a house or move — do we both respect each other's access to revelation? When a woman feels inspired to adjust her life — does she feel like she needs to get permission or can she follow her inspiration?

A sovereign woman trusts the revelation God gives her ... and actively seeks it. If we simply default to what tradition or culture or humans say — we are not being sovereign beings.

> **Until recently, we taught that women have a mediated relationship to God. This has changed in our temple worship ... but has it changed in our default settings?**

My most powerful experience of learning sovereignty was the process of divining God's will in who I should marry and create life with. I fasted and prayed weekly for a year to know if marrying my not-of-our-faith man was the person I should marry. The laceration of trying to reconcile the consistent minor miracles that kept putting me back on the marriage path with all of the commandments and teachings and family culture and, and, and ... was brutal. The cognitive dissonance almost tore me apart. In the end, I got the most clear answer to prayer I've ever received ... it was God's will that I marry this man who was not of my faith. I developed a deepened relationship with God. And I gained a rock solid testimony of the necessity of being a spiritually sovereign being.

ETERNAL PROTOTYPE

It IS a scarier, more demanding path to always align ourselves with God's will, to always turn to God before we turn to any other sources. But the possibility of our destiny of godhood demands it.

God is the ultimate authority ... and we must stretch our agency muscles over and over again to become like Them. We need practice!

> "Now you know a very small part of what I feel for each of these my children, as their Mother."

THE point of earth life is to become sovereign beings. (And perhaps not judge others on their sovereign paths.)

What can you do today to become a more sovereign being?

3- Eternal Prototype Means Learning to Love The Other

When I give Heavenly Mother firesides, women often come up to me and ask if they can tell me their story of Heavenly Mother. I always say yes ... but I also realize my perimenopausal brain is not a reliable repository to keep these. After one particularly compelling story, we decided to create the Cherish books. (And through divine guidance the three of us connected!) You can find this story and many others in the two volumes, but today, I want to tell you one story that feels particularly applicable now.

A woman had been diligently praying that she would be able to learn to love those different from her. She was having a hard time loving her neighbors who thought and felt and voted so differently than she did. As she was standing in the pharmacy aisle of Walmart in Rexburg, Idaho, she felt a growing awareness of all the people in the store: a man was back buying a fishing pole in one corner and toddler was having a meltdown in aisle 37 and a mother was fretting about expenses as she took her children school clothes shopping. As the woman became aware of every person in that Walmart, she felt an overwhelming sense of deep and all-encompassing love for each of them. A voice came into her mind, "Now you know a very small part of what I feel for each of these my children, as their Mother."

> **It IS a scarier, more demanding path to always align ourselves with God's will, to always turn to God before we turn to any other sources. But the possibility of our destiny of godhood demands it.**

The truth the restored gospel offers is that we are all part of a Heavenly Family.

We need each other ... maybe especially those who are difficult for us. Those interactions can provide the rub that helps us refine ourselves to ever grow more Christlike in our choices.

The third reason we need to acknowledge Heavenly Mother as our prototype is that She models a perfect mother love for all Her children ... even those so very different from us.

My youngest daughter often plays the "I love you," "I love you more," "I love you best" game up to ever increasing heights until one of us hits, "I love you like God." And THAT is the truth — God loves best... and that can give mortal mothers a reassurance. When I am not perfect (duh), I can trust my Mother can love my children perfectly.

ALL of us have times when we simply need our Mother's love.

Bottom Line — Women Matter

If we teach that Heavenly Mother matters, we teach that women matter.

Mary Daly famously said, "when god is male, male is god." Now, we believe from our theology that Heavenly Father did not become God on His own ... which means a single male is not supreme by himself. We know this. But when we mistakenly adopt a fallen world's model ... then we tangle up the divine order. We have rarely modeled men and women working together as full partners ... but that's our belief in the divine pattern!

One of the exciting parts of the Gospel Topics essay is that the existence of Heavenly Mother reorders our priorities from a male only supreme being to a joint partnership — and that eternal prototype trickles down into every aspect of life.

> **If we teach that Heavenly Mother matters, we teach that women matter.**

The existence of Heavenly Mother reorders the entire world. And THAT is vital.

SOURCES

1 Michael Goodman, associate professor of Church history and doctrine, Brigham Young University. "The Powerful Doctrine of Eternal Marriage," Education Week presentation.
2 Dieter F. Uchtdorf, "Three Sisters," October 2017 general conference.
3 Terryl Givens, "How Free Is Your Will? A Conversation with Terryl Givens," Faith Matters podcast, February 8, 2025, faithmatters.org/category/podcasts/.

THE MISSING PIECE
Michael Workman

My wife's journey to discover Heavenly Mother initially frightened me, but I came to realize that I was making her spiritual journey more about myself. What did her search mean for our relationship? How might it affect her connection to the Church and, by extension, our place within it? Ultimately, it was all about me — how was this going to affect me?

At first, I reconciled these questions with the knowledge that Heavenly Mother is part of our doctrine. It was acceptable to explore doctrine, even if "She is too sacred to be talked about." Ironically, that very idea pushed me to question it more. Thus, I turned to the words of the prophets, searched the scriptures, and studied history to understand whether there was any legitimacy to this belief, and how or why She had been banished from our collective awareness. But ultimately, I did what we emphasize as the most vital practice of our faith: I prayed and sought to know for myself.

> *Now, it is profoundly beautiful to know that I have a Mother in Heaven.*

As a bomb technician for the U.S. military, I have received extensive training in analytical problem-solving and emotionless decision-making. However, after exhausting those means in my search for Heavenly Mother and Her place in my theological framework, it ultimately came down to knowing through faith, hope, and prayer. The confirmation that came through the Spirit has been more enriching than any other endeavor on the matter.

Now, it is profoundly beautiful to know that I have a Mother in Heaven. She, like my Father in Heaven, is aware of and active in my life. She is part of the model that my wife and I can embody in divine partnership by becoming one flesh. In addition, my daughter can now see herself reflected more in her own plan of salvation. Understanding Heavenly Mother was the missing piece in my view of the heavenly family — because how could I ever become like God without Her?

IN HER LOVE

There's a voice I'm coming to know
A Mother's love that helps me grow
Heavenly Mother, full of grace
In Her arms, I've found my place
Like my mother here below
Her love shows me where to go
In Her care, I start to see
Who I am, who I can be

In Her love, I find my way
Her gentle light guides my day
With Heavenly Parents, I'm whole
Their love heals my soul
As I know Her heart so true
I learn to love me too
Heaven's child, I'm meant to be
In Her love, I find me

She knows the pain I face each day
Her Son lifts me when I pray
She shows me love that never ends

In Her light, my heart mends
Just like my mother here on earth
She reminds me of my worth

ETERNAL PROTOTYPE

Her love eternal, pure and bright
In Her warmth, I find my light
In Her love, I find my way
Her gentle light guides my day
With Heavenly Parents, I'm whole
Their love heals my soul
As I know Her heart so true
I learn to love me too
Heaven's child, I'm meant to be
In Her love, I find me

With my Father by Her side
She helps me see what's deep inside
In Her grace, I start to see
The beauty She's placed in me

In Her love, I find my way
Her gentle light guides my day
With Heavenly Parents, I'm whole
Their love heals my soul

As I know Her heart so true
I learn to love me too
Heaven's child, I'm meant to be
In Her love, I find me

With Heavenly Mother, I'm free
In Her love, I find me

STUDY HELPS
Eternal Prototype

"Mother in Heaven" Gospel Topics essay footnotes

Footnote 13: "Our Mother in Heaven," Latter-day Saints' Millennial Star 72, no. 39 (Sept. 29, 1910): 620. By Elder Rudger Clawson.

Study 1

> "Eternal: (adj) incessant, God. Prototype: (n) the original form, pattern, model."
> —Webster's Handy College Dictionary (1972, p.164, 366)

> "Eternal: (adj) everlasting, perpetual. Prototype: (n) original model, archetype."
> —The Merriam-Webster Dictionary (2022, p.248, 589)

Using these definitions, how would you describe the Eternal Mother?

The definition of prototype is an original pattern, form, and model. What makes Heavenly Mother a prototype? How do we become an actual model built from that prototype?

Because we are made in Heavenly Mother's image, does that make us a prototype? Why or why not?

Study 2

In Hebrew, one of the words for God is "Elohim," which can be understood to be plural, male and female depending on context. (If you want to dig in, get an interlinear Hebrew Bible and you can key word search "Elohim" to see all references. There are over 2500 but not all refer to Heavenly Mother and Father.)

According to the Gospel Topics Essay, The Divine pattern that has been set for us is not a supreme male god but a Heavenly Father and a Heavenly Mother working together as full partners. How does knowing this reorder the world for you?

Where have you seen effective examples of joint partnership? What do they look like? How do they function?

ETERNAL PROTOTYPE

Where would you like to see more examples of joint partnership? What would that look like? How would that change things?

Study 3

> President Spencer W. Kimball supposed that our renewed relationship with our Heavenly Mother would be immensely influential. He reasoned, "Knowing how profoundly our mortal mothers have shaped us here, do we suppose her influence on us as individuals to be less if we live so as to return [to heaven]?" Accordingly, the loving support and example of both Father and Mother will guide us in the eternities. [1]

How do you invest in your soul?

How do you cultivate becoming a sovereign being?

Suggested Reading

"Mother," Amanda Jenkins, *Cherish* book 1, p. 370.
"Look in a Mirror," Lorraine Pemberton, *Cherish* book 2, p. 420-421.
"Be Ye Therefore Perfect," Ashli Carnicelli, *Cherish* book 1, p. 346.

1 Paulsen, "A Mother There," p.16.

11. SACRED KNOWLEDGE

"As with many other truths of the gospel, our present knowledge
about a Mother in Heaven is limited. Nevertheless, we have
been given sufficient **knowledge** to
appreciate the **sacredness** of this doctrine."

Mother in Heaven essay, paragraph 6

GATHERING INTELLIGENCE

> And I give unto you a commandment that you shall teach one another the doctrine of the kingdom. Teach ye diligently and my grace shall attend you, that you may be instructed more perfectly in theory, in principle, in doctrine, in the law of the gospel, in all things that pertain unto the kingdom of God, that are expedient for you to understand; Of things both in heaven and in the earth, and under the earth; things which have been, things which are, things which must shortly come to pass; things which are at home, things which are abroad; the wars and perplexities of the nations, and the judgments which are on the land; and a knowledge also of countries and of kingdoms— That ye may be prepared in all things when I shall send you again to magnify the calling whereunto I have called you, and the mission with which I have commissioned you. — Doctrine and Covenants 88: 77-80

> Whatever principle of intelligence we attain unto in this life, it will rise with us in the resurrection. And if a person gains more knowledge and intelligence in this life through his diligence and obedience than another, he will have so much the advantage in the world to come. — Doctrine and Covenants 130: 18-19

The origin story of the Church of Jesus Christ of Latter-day Saints begins with a question — what do I do with this situation in my life? God's answer, then and now, is the same: "If any of you lack wisdom, let him ask of God." (James 1:5)

Modern businesses frequently train their employees to use the DIKW pyramid: Data, Information, Knowledge, Wisdom.

- Data: raw facts

- Information: the organization of facts to analyze and learn from

- Knowledge: the amalgamation of multiple blocks of information, gaining deeper insights, the sum total of education

- Wisdom: the application of data, information, and knowledge into our actions and behaviors

Intelligence is perhaps the integration of our knowledge and wisdom with our hearts and souls.

SACRED KNOWLEDGE

As prophets and apostles receive revelation and declare doctrine, we individually incorporate that information into our knowledge and decide how it should be applied to our specific circumstances. The Gospel Topics essay, "Mother in Heaven," is one such example of Latter-day Saint leaders issuing a doctrinal statement for Latter-day Saints to gain information and knowledge, and turn it into wisdom for their lives.

Marjorie Pay Hinckley, President Hinckley's dear wife, expressed delight at gaining spiritual knowledge: "The beautiful thing — perhaps the thing I love most about the gospel — is that everything we learn we can use and take with us and use it again. No bit of knowledge goes wasted. Everything you are learning now is preparing you for something else. Did you know that? What a concept!"

"DIKW Pyramid," Wikipedia December 20, 2024, en.wikipedia.org/wiki/DIKW_pyramid
Marjorie Pay Hinckley, Small and Simple Things (Salt Lake City: Deseret Book, 2003), p. 138.

THE GARDEN

Lucy Mason

A GOOD CROP:
CULTIVATING OUR DOCTRINE OF A HEAVENLY MOTHER

Patrick Q. Mason

Several years ago, I taught a graduate seminar on Mormonism and gender. It was one of the most memorable teaching experiences of my career. There were about a dozen of us in the room, ranging from lifelong devout Latter-day Saints to agnostic LGBTQ activists. As we read and talked about polygamy, patriarchy, and male-only priesthood, let's just say the secular progressives in the class were not exactly lining up to be baptized. Then, near the end of the semester, I assigned a set of readings about Heavenly Mother. When I walked into the classroom that week, the mood was completely different. The non-LDS students exclaimed, "Why have you been holding out on us? Mormonism has a Heavenly Mother and you didn't tell us about Her until now? This is amazing! This should be the first thing the Church tells people!"

None of those students converted to the Church of Jesus Christ of Latter-day Saints. But they were completely smitten with the idea of a Mother in Heaven. As graduate students in religious studies, they were aware of the "divine feminine" that exists in different religious traditions but they were particularly drawn in by how personal, intimate, and empowering the Latter-day Saint doctrine of Heavenly Mother felt. To this group of students—who could all quote Mary Daly's insight that "If God is male, then the male is God" [1] — it simply felt right to think of God as the exalted partnership of the divine masculine and feminine, or Father and Mother. This was a God they could believe in.

> "Why have you been holding out on us? Mormonism has a Heavenly Mother and you didn't tell us about Her until now? This is amazing! This should be the first thing the Church tells people!"

Heavenly Mother is Latter-day Saints' best-kept secret that should not be a secret. On its official website, the Church affirms that "the doctrine of a Heavenly Mother is a cherished and distinctive belief among Latter-day Saints." [2] However, the relative silence and general discomfort around our Mother in Heaven calls into question just how well we have collectively stewarded this "cherished and distinctive belief."

In my book Restoration, I reflected on a metaphor of the world as a garden or farm in which grows every good gift from God. [3] The garden is far too big for any one group to tend all by themselves, so God has assigned different groups to specialize in caring for certain crops. Buddhists, it seems to me, have done an extraordinary job cultivating contemplative practices.

Jews have shown us what it means to be a chosen people in service of humanity. Muslims have emphasized the oneness of God, while Hindus have reveled in God's many faces. Secular humanists have leaned into our profound capacity for reason and the importance of human rights. Within the sprawling Christian section of the garden, Catholics have tended to tradition and mystery, evangelicals have nurtured grace, and Pentecostals have reminded us all that worship

> **Whether out of uncertainty, fear, or an overabundance of reverent caution, we have been stingy with our doctrine of a Heavenly Mother.**

is meant to be joyous and Spirit-filled. None of these fruits are designed to be hoarded. A certain person or group might be called to cultivate a particular crop, but "all these gifts come from God, for the benefit of the children of God." [4] Having been lovingly nurtured, our gifts are meant to be distributed widely.

Latter-day Saints make up only a tiny sliver of the laborers in God's garden. But just as with the other religions, God has entrusted us with some distinctive crops to plant, tend, harvest, and share. Among these tasty fruits are the Book of Mormon, living prophets and apostles, and eternal marriage. Another one of the genuinely important crops that God has given Latter-day Saints to cultivate is our knowledge that we have "a Mother there." [5] Joseph Smith taught that "there are but very few beings in the world who understand rightly the character of God," and that if people "do not comprehend the character of God they do not comprehend their own character." [6] Helping our sisters and brothers around the world understand that godhood consists of a Father and Mother united for all eternity will help them comprehend not only the character of God but also who they are and are destined to become.

Jesus taught that the kingdom of God is like a sumptuous feast that all are invited to. Some of the banquet's offerings will be more enticing to certain people at certain times. [7] Our mantra as a missionary church is to preach the gospel to anyone who will listen, then respect their agency as they decide whether they will embrace our teachings. We have flooded the earth with the Book of Mormon. Yet we have dammed up the doctrine of a Heavenly Mother so that only a trickle of life-giving water has flowed from this particular reservoir of faith. While no latter-day prophet or apostle has ever said that we should drain the reservoir, some well-meaning Church members have suggested that the water is not safe to drink from or deep enough to swim in. [8] Whether out of uncertainty, fear, or an overabundance of reverent caution, we have been stingy with our doctrine of a Heavenly Mother. We have withheld this glorious doctrine of the Restoration that could heal hearts, enlighten minds, and nourish souls. We can do more to invite all of God's children to the feast of our Father's and Mother's love.

One of the most radical things we believe as Latter-day Saints is also one of the simplest. Every time a new mother or father sings "I Am a Child of God" to their babe-in-arms, and every time Primary children melt our hearts with those lyrics, we affirm the Restoration's most world-changing teaching: You and I and every human being on this planet is literally a spirit daughter or son of Heavenly Parents. There is perhaps no group of people I admire more than single parents. But most of them would say they are single parenting out of circumstance and necessity, not out of choice. Our Father is not a single parent; the very thought of an Eternal Father without a Mother "makes reason stare." [9] So when we sing "Am a Child of God," we are testifying of both a Mother and Father in Heaven. President Dallin H. Oaks has affirmed that "Our theology begins with Heavenly Parents." [10] Everything in the restored gospel flows from that basic and glorious fact.

What makes this doctrine so radical is not just its novelty but its ethical imperative. In other words, believing that every person is a child of Heavenly Parents is not just a theological abstraction — it has consequences for how we conduct ourselves in the world. C.S. Lewis wrote that "next to the Blessed Sacrament itself, your neighbor is the holiest object presented to your senses." [11] Because Latter-day Saints believe that God is symbolically but not actually present in the sacramental emblems, we can shorten Lewis's poignant observation, leaving out the first clause and simply stating, "your neighbor is the holiest object presented to your senses." Why? Because your neighbor — that person butting in line, or voting for the "wrong" candidate, or whose comments in church drive you crazy, or whom you married or gave birth to — is literally the offspring and heir of God, our Eternal Father and Mother. If we really believed that, if we really taught it, if we really lived it, it would change everything: the way we do business, the way we show up in our communities (religious and secular), the way we approach politics, the way we relate to our family members. I've said or done my fair share of rude or downright mean things to other people that I would have never said or done if their mother was in the room. When we think of God only as a sovereign Creator, we can look at the people around us as mere creatures. But when we think of God first and foremost as a divine Father and Mother, we begin to see the people around us — Their children — as family. When we plant the doctrine of Heavenly Mother deep in our hearts, it changes the way we treat the rest of Her children.

> **Believing that every person is a child of Heavenly Parents is not just a theological abstraction - it has consequences for how we conduct ourselves in the world.**

> We don't have to be perfectly knowledgeable horticulturalists. God just asks us to be willing gardeners.

I close with a confession. I don't fully know how to plant, nurture, sustain, and harvest our doctrine of a Mother in Heaven. With some of the other crops that God has asked the Latter-day Saints to attend, we have been given lengthy growing guides (we call them scriptures). We have a fair bit of experience now with the Book of Mormon, though it is still surprising us with its seemingly endless bounties. Millions of families can testify of the good fruits that stem from the sealing ordinance. But because we have largely left the seeds in the packet, we are still in the early phases of figuring out how to cultivate our belief in a Heavenly Mother. Which soils are most conducive to its growth? Does it prefer sun or shade? What kind of pruning helps it thrive? How does it cross-fertilize with other plants? What pests do we need to watch out for that could damage the crop? The only way to know, as Alma counseled us with any true doctrine of the gospel, will be to experiment — to plant the seed, care for it, and watch it sprout and grow. [12] We don't have to be perfectly knowledgeable horticulturalists. God just asks us to be willing gardeners.

SOURCES

1 Mary Daly, Beyond God the Father: Toward a Philosophy of Women's Liberation (Boston: Beacon Press, 1973), 19.
2 "Mother in Heaven," Gospel Topics essays, churchofjesuschrist.org/study/manual/gospel-topics-essays.
3 Patrick Q. Mason, Restoration: God's Call to the 21st-Century World (Meridian, ID: Faith Matters, 2020), 46-48.
4 Doctrine & Covenants 46:26.
5 Eliza R. Snow, "O My Father," LDS Hymnal, (Salt Lake City, UT: The Church of Jesus Christ of Latter-day Saints, 1981), 292.
6 Joseph Smith, in Stan Larsen, "The King Follett Discourse: A Newly Amalgamated Text," BYU Studies Quarterly 18:2 (April 1978): 199.
7 See Matthew 22:1-14.
8 See David L. Paulsen and Martin Pulido, "'A Mother There': A Survey of Historical Teachings about Mother in Heaven," BYU Studies Quarterly 50:1 (2011): 71-97.
9 "O My Father"
10 Dallin H. Oaks, "Apostasy and Restoration," Ensign, May 1995, 84.
11 C.S. Lewis, The Weight of Glory: And Other Addresses (1949; reprinted San Francisco: HarperCollins, 2001), 46.
12 See Alma 32:27-36.

SACRED KNOWLEDGE

STUDY HELPS
Sacred Knowledge

"Mother in Heaven" Gospel Topics essay footnote

Footnote 14: 1 Corinthians 11:11.

Study 1

> "Knowledge: (n) awareness of facts, truths, or principles; cognizance; erudition; a body of accumulated facts. Sacred: (adj.) dedicated to deity; holy; invariable (not be violated). —Webster's Handy College Dictionary (1972)

> "Knowledge: understanding gained in actual experience; range of information; something learned and kept in the mind. Sacred knowledge: set apart for the service or worship of deity; devoted exclusively; worthy of reverence." —The Merriam-Webster Dictionary (2022)

What information or knowledge of facts, truths, or principles do you know about Heavenly Mother that makes this knowledge sacred?

Using this definition of sacred, why is our knowledge of Heavenly Mother considered sacred?

What is your own definition of sacred knowledge pertaining to Heavenly Mother? Why is this sacred, and not just information?

Study 2

> There is not a greater and more glorious set of promises given than those which come through the gospel. ... Where else can you learn who you are? Where else can you learn the necessary explanations and assurances about the nature of life? From what other sources can you learn about your uniqueness and identity? — President Spencer W. Kimball [1]

How do you know who you really are?

How did you learn the nature of life?

What is your true identity?

What unique characteristics do you have that you feel come from your Heavenly Parents?

What sacred knowledge have you gained through your patriarchal blessing about your true identity and unique characteristics? How is this blessing a guiding influence in your life?

Study 3

> This does not mean that we claim sufficient spiritual maturity to comprehend God. ... But we can comprehend the fundamentals He has revealed about Himself and other members of the Godhead. And that knowledge is essential to our understanding of the purpose of mortal life and our eternal destiny as resurrected beings after mortal life. ... The theology of the restored Church of Jesus Christ, the purpose of mortal life is to prepare us to realize our destiny as sons and daughters of God. — Elder Dallin H. Oaks [2]

What are fundamental principles that have been revealed about Heavenly Father and other members of the Godhead?

What does spiritual maturity mean to you in relationship to Heavenly Mother?

What knowledge and understanding of our purpose of mortal life and eternal destiny is taught in the Restored Gospel?

How has your understanding of sacred knowledge become clearer after studying these concepts?

How can your knowledge be shared with others to help them understand the sacredness of the doctrine of Heavenly Mother?

Suggested Reading

"Heavenly Mother Wisdom," Malinda Wagstaff, *Cherish* book 1, p. 391
"Divine Esteem," Shima Baughman, *Cherish* book 1, p. 394

1 President Spencer W. Kimball, "The Role of Righteous Women," Improvement Era, November 1979.
2 Elder Dallin H. Oaks, "Apostasy and Restoration," April 1995 general conference.

12. HIGHEST ASPIRATION

"As Elder Dallin H. Oaks of the Quorum of the Twelve Apostles has said, 'Our theology begins with Heavenly Parents. Our **highest aspiration** is to be like Them'."

Mother in Heaven essay, paragraph 6

THE BEST VERSION OF OURSELVES

In the Gospel Topics essay, "Mother in Heaven," President Oaks explains what all this messy, chaotic, challenging, invigorating, and luscious life experience is for: to BE LIKE THEM.

The kaleidoscope of the world, with the myriad of experiences and challenges and relationships, can still drill down to the core of the gospel, the core of this life: to develop and grow and become an eternal family with our current earthly families as well as with our eternal Heavenly Parents.

> We each belong to and are needed in the family of God. — Carole M. Stephens

Prophets and other church leaders across time have spoken of godly characteristics that we develop in our own lives and selves, including becoming creators.

> We are all creators. ... Creation is one of the characteristics that defines God. Brothers and sisters, we are children of God. Shouldn't we be creators as well? You might say, "I'm not creative." I'm here to tell you, you are. You are creators. Have you ever coaxed a smile from a baby? Have you ever taught someone to forgive? Have you helped someone learn to read? Prepared a family home evening? Organized a family reunion? Possibly you were prompted to do something for a person you go visiting teaching or home teaching to that made a great difference in their lives. If you have done some of these things, you have been creative. — President Mary Ellen Smoot

Our lives are the most important creation we will do. In creating the best version of ourselves, we advance the plan of our Heavenly Parents.

Carole M. Stephens, Relief Society general presidency counselor, 2012-17, "The Family is of God," April 2015 general conference.
President Mary Ellen Smoot, Relief Society general president, 1997-2002, "We Are Creators," April 2000 general conference.

THE GEM OF THE RESTORATION
Bethany Brady Spalding and Andy Brady Spalding

Our theology **begins** with Heavenly Parents. Our highest **aspiration** is to be like Them. — Dallin H. Oaks

First up, Bethany ...

Our theology begins with Heavenly Parents, and our rigorous romance actually did too. There we were — a Mormon girl and a Methodist boy — gazing up at the towering, coral sandstone cliffs of Capitol Reef National Park — trying to navigate a budding relationship that felt full of grand potential but fraught with possible problems too: our different faith traditions being first and foremost.

Andy had a deep and probing spiritual curiosity that had drawn him to the LDS faith many times throughout his life ... in high school, graduate school, law school, and legal clerkship. He had studied the Book of Mormon, scoured Talmage's Articles of Faith, watched general conference, and delved into doctrine with missionaries. But it wasn't until that night — sitting under the stars together while the moonlight danced on the red rock walls — that the most sublime truths of the restored gospel resonated with his searching soul. And what did it? A simple introduction to our theology of Heavenly Parents.

A wave of inspiration struck me in our Capitol Reef campground, and I posed these provocative questions: Can you imagine that all of this stunning landscape was sculpted by two passionate lovers — a Heavenly Father and a Heavenly Mother? And all for the purpose of creating a place where Their children could learn to love as They do? Can you conceive that all of these magnificent domes and twisting canyons and exquisite arches are the handiwork of a coupled God? ... And the very essence of Godhood is passionate partnership and co-creation?

These theological questions lit Andy on fire! He was ready to dive into this religion and romance.

The ultimate aim of the restored gospel — with its emphasis on marriage, family, temples, sealings, eternal progression, and infinite relationships — was not completely cohesive and compelling to Andy until he understood the theology of Heavenly Parents. Why did it take him almost twenty years of exploring Mormonism to encounter this life-altering truth? Elder Oaks teaches that our theology begins with Heavenly Parents, so why was it just about the last thing he learned?

That late night conversation in Capitol Reef changed the trajectory of our lives and sparked some big questions in my heart: Why don't all gospel conversations begin with the celebratory truths that we are beloved children of Heavenly Parents? Why do we insist on hiding this light under a bushel, instead of letting it gloriously shine?

Why don't Latter-day Saints shout this gem of the Restoration from the rooftops? Why don't we desire for every inhabitant of this hungry world to know that God is a couple, that equality is divine, and that partnership is the very essence of Godhood? These delicious truths transform people and open boundless possibilities.

Next up, Andy ...

The word "aspire" fits so very well in a conversation about partnership. To spiritually aspire, it seems, is to reach continuously towards something that feels just beyond our grasp — some kind of intimation, a flicker of a conviction located somewhere deep within, that there simply must be something better than whatever we have known, or seen, or inherited.

Divine and eternal equality in partnership is this kind of aspiration. Well, it is when you're married to someone like my present co-author: a truly visionary woman who sees divine potential in others and in the world as very few do or ever have; who can always see the person in front of her as the most important person on the planet; whose every fiber of being longs for all that is "virtuous, lovely, or of good report or praiseworthy" and who is deeply repulsed by the menial, the crude, or the false; and in whose every movement and word seems to "sing the song of redeeming love" (Alma 5:26).

> **The ultimate aim of the restored gospel — with its emphasis on marriage, family, temples, sealings, eternal progression, and infinite relationships — was not completely cohesive and compelling to Andy until he understood the theology of Heavenly Parents.**

Whew, that's a lot. Indeed, after Bethany's and my first date twenty years ago, my sisters asked me, "so how was it?" I stared into the distance and replied, "I'm afraid I'm not her equal." My sisters loved to hear it. Soon thereafter I loved, and aspired to an equal partnership with Bethany. If I'm being honest, I still aspire. I've seen equality without deep partnership, and deep partnership without equality. Our distinctive LDS hope is to somehow realize them both.

> **As I aspire to be her equal – agreeing to alternately teach and be taught, lead and be led – she becomes as a midwife to my own inner Christ-like nature, despite or perhaps because of the pangs of birth.**

To aspire is to look beyond the past and the present, and sometimes even beyond the limitations of the scriptures themselves. Paul's oft-quoted passage from Ephesians 5 about husbands loving their wives as Christ loves the church completely neglects, quite conspicuously, to describe a comparably Christ-like vision for women. So too in the following chapter does he describe how fathers ought to be Christ-like toward their children, with no mention of motherhood. It seems the eternal nature and destiny of women, and the divine model of marriage, simply were not this unmarried apostle's forte. Very well. Through modern revelation we learn to be no more constrained by his time-bound teachings on marriage than his teachings in the same chapters on slavery. Two thousand years later, we are resolute in abolishing Paul's master-slave hierarchy, and still growing into a resolution to abolish the husband-wife hierarchy. The model of Heavenly Parents compels us to let that hierarchy go.

In chapter 9 of this book, Thomas McConkie invokes a metaphor that originates elsewhere in the Abrahamic faiths but aligns with our LDS theology of Heavenly Parents: an ancient name for God, Ya Rahman, which translates as "womb." The imagery is evocative. Maybe my extraordinary wife and I are now, in this mortal realm, as two fetuses in a shared womb, turning, twisting, and kicking, longing to be born beyond the veil into an eternal dimension of light, learning, and more perfectly-loving partnership. Will it all be easier on the other side? Maybe and maybe not. But in those still and peaceful moments, I find inspiration in knowing that my spouse is created in the likeness of God. Because she is, it simply must be that a gendered God is not exclusively male. I know that my companionship with a woman who bears divinity in her strength, vision, and heart has been the greatest blessing of my life.

And I know that as I aspire to be her equal – agreeing to alternately teach and be taught, lead and be led – she becomes as a midwife to my own inner Christ-like nature, despite or perhaps because of the pangs of birth.

Back to Bethany ...

Yes — partnership is holy work, but it sure is damn hard. As a fiercely independent free spirit who prefers to tackle things on my own, couplehood hasn't come easy for me. Andy — on the other hand — is wired for emotional intimacy and was born to partner. I am a slow learner but know deep down that I am a fuller person when I can lean into his distinctive strengths. He has been a patient teacher and continues to forgive my missteps two decades into this forever marriage experiment. Over the wild ride of twenty years, we've aspired to partner in parenting: co-creating and co-nurturing three phenomenal girls together. We've aspired to partner at church: co-directing a ward tutoring program for urban youth; co-running a rambunctious, bilingual Primary; and co-leading a prison ministry in our stake. We've aspired to partner in providing: each using our unique capacities to create resources and experiences for our family.

> *It has been the theology of Heavenly Parents that keeps drawing us towards an expansive view of the eternal potential of our partnership.*

As Andy and I discovered our vast differences while we were dating, we came to the stark realization that our differences had the potential to expand us or crush us. And while we've both certainly felt crushed at times, it has been the theology of Heavenly Parents that keeps drawing us towards an expansive view of the eternal potential of our partnership. So we keep striving, hoping, healing, and visiting red rock canyons to remember the foundational truths of our relationship: Our theology begins with Heavenly Parents. Our highest aspiration is to be like Them - partnered, powerful, passionately loving, creative, endless.

HIGHEST ASPIRATION

THE THRONE OF GOD

Ginger Dall Egbert

BECOMING GODLIKE IS NOW

Aubrey Chaves

McArthur Krishna interviewed Aubrey Chaves in December 2024 about seeking our highest aspiration to be like our Heavenly Parents. This is an excerpt of their conversation. The full transcript is published on HeavenlyMotherMatters.org and the podcast video can be found on Faith Matters YouTube channel.

McArthur Krishna: When we talk about becoming Godlike, "our highest aspiration is to be like Them," somehow it feels in that language that it's far off. Perfection is far off. But instead of thinking of it in terms that are out ahead of us, which is maybe less productive, everything we've been talking about is that becoming Godlike is now: processing now, thinking through now, acknowledging our gifts now, wrestling now. So my question is with "highest aspiration," how do you understand "becoming Godlike "– the idea of functioning in yourself, in the world, in the people you love? How is that functioning now?

Aubrey Chaves: That's such an interesting question. When I imagine something so far, far away, it's a way of not having to do a hard thing. It's almost a relief to say "someday" to get out of the work of the moment. When I think of "our highest aspiration is to be like Them," in a really present way, it gives me clarity about what is right in front of me.

If I'm having an interaction with one of my kids that is bringing out the worst in myself, in that experience I want to say, "This is hard and someday I'll figure it out." But the idea that we're practicing to be like our Heavenly Parents gives me clarity for what to do in this exact moment. What does infinite love look like in this difficult interaction, where it feels like love is the exception? There's something hard, I don't feel qualified, and I don't know what to do. But having this thought of our Heavenly Parents present in my mind puts into focus that the only thing that matters is love.

It gets complicated when love is moved far away – I'm thinking about the books I've read, the thing that happened yesterday, blood sugar ... everything gets so complicated. I like having the present goal to embody love that is genuinely overwhelming and unconditional. I know what's hard in the moment, and I don't know what it would be like to be God.

> **But the idea that we're practicing to be like our Heavenly Parents gives me clarity for what to do in this exact moment.**

The best I can do is imagine what unconditional love looks like in this moment. I think that's the real point of this life — to have a million of those moments, practicing embodying that love. We get different flavors of it in every context of our life. But it's always going to be about a complete presence in the moment that's right in front of us.

MK: That's incredibly beautiful. Trying to have a highest aspiration now makes it in some ways less daunting. Do you have tips or ideas of how to live into your highest aspiration? I always think that women especially need soul investment. That seems to be an important angle — that there's a gap between us and God. If we're going to become more Godlike, we have to grow and develop. Different life experiences give us different growth.

Becoming a mother was one of the most clarifying moments. I was a stepmother before I was a biological mother, and even that was a clarifying moment of saying, there's a being in this universe that demands my best self and their needs outrank mine. I'm not saying a mother's needs never matter. But there's a difference between what a child can grasp and what an adult can grasp. If I'm hungry and they're hungry, I can understand what's going on, I can pause and manage.

> *I always think that women especially need soul investment. That seems to be an important angle — that there's a gap between us and God. If we're going to become more Godlike, we have to grow and develop.*

AC: As soon as you started the question, I thought of what you've taught me about soul investment. I'm glad that's where you took it because in real life, that has been the most consistent way I've found what's next for me, the next place I need to grow. I'll just be specific:

Almost ten years ago, I started baking. I've always loved baking but I started decorating cakes, making wedding cakes and crazy special event cakes. It was a random thing I felt so drawn to and it felt like spiritual work. I have to own that — my soul really needed this thing. I was a mom and slipping very easily into a life framework that said it would be better to ignore my wants and needs. We had four little kids and ignoring my needs was becoming a habit and I could feel my soul trying to break out. I needed space to spread out and be creative.

MK: I want to pause because I think there are Godlike things to be learning. Christ sacrificed for us — there's something to be learned in being willing to sacrifice for another human being. I don't want to denigrate that. Being a full-time busy mom to little kids gives a whole new level of being Godlike. And there are other paths, and other necessary developments. That can't be the only Godlike attribute.

AC: That's why I like that you called it soul investment. Had I started when we got married and I was cake-decorating full time and living a wildly creative life, doing what I really enjoy, I think I would have come along to this point where I thought, I want to take care of something. I want to give in another way and I can feel my soul reaching for that.

I was at a point where my soul felt out of balance, and the antidote I could sense I needed was deep creativity. "Soul investment" is the perfect catch-all because it's about sensing exactly what your soul needs.

> I was at a point where my soul felt out of balance, and the antidote I could sense I needed was deep creativity.

That's going to look different in every context. In my context, ten years ago, it looked like, "You're drying up." I needed something that felt nourishing and spiritual. It was practice to recognize what I liked, and building a skill that was really just for my own spiritual expansion. It felt so nourishing to create something and find it beautiful, and do it again and again, and just have time alone. I would do it in the middle of the night. I needed silence, and I needed to make a lot of decisions that were just for me.

Then it was nourishing to ask to be compensated for it. It was all uncomfortable and totally nourishing growth. So I like this idea of soul investment. If I'd had language for it then, it would have been an easier adjustment. I could have said, "Okay, I can feel I need some development here. So I'm going all in and it is worthwhile." It felt more like a wrestle to me — is it okay that I'm doing this? Why am I doing it? Is it okay for someone else to sacrifice so I can do it? I felt uneasy in the beginning. But years later, I can see how this was the tool my soul could work with. God was using the tool of baking to help me grow in a specific way—it helped me find and develop a much healthier and stronger sense of self. That has become my container.

It's the reason the Faith Matters podcast works, because I can find my questions, and my pain and fear. Those were getting set aside so they were hard to locate. Baking and decorating beautiful wedding cakes was the way I reconnected with a deep sense of self, and I have found more than anything else, it has been the most important way to connect with God.

HIGHEST ASPIRATION

I had to find a sense of self so I could hear God. When I was trying to be translucent and a helper, it was getting so hard to find that inner compass. I don't understand how these things are so connected, I just know that they are. The fruit of staying up late and making cakes by myself is that I can feel where my soul wants to go now. It has turned me toward my family. It has been a deeply centering experiment.

> **I had to find a sense of self so I could hear God.**

So soul investment is the "boots on the ground" reality to answer all of these questions. I had to do that first. I had to believe that there was something worthwhile to give time and energy and respect to. I had to figure out how to honor it, so I could hear it.

MK: I am so delighted! God has never spoken to me through baking, but that's exactly what we're talking about. The human soul is infinite, and this is how God was able to expand your soul. Think about the virtuous cycle you were describing — when you invested in your soul, that led you to be more yourself. Becoming the best version of ourselves is the whole point! There was more Happy Aubrey to give to your family and it took you to an even better place. Abundance!

AC: I love that one of the few things we know about God is They create! Maybe it's not baking ... but there is genuinely something about ways to be creative. It could be so many different things you might not recognize it as creativity. There's something about the kind of stretching and reaching we have to do in creativity that makes us sensitive to God's voice. That reaching works across the board — feeling for what would work. It feels similar to feeling for the energy that is directing me. There's something special and Godlike about practicing creativity. That by itself is a spiritual tool.

> **I love that one of the few things we know about God is They create!**

MK: My mom just told me a story this morning about creativity. She told me about a class at BYU when she was twenty-something, married, pregnant with me, and the professor said to the class, "Do you think you're creative?" Most of the people in the room said they were not creative, including my mom. The professor said, "Your assignment is to walk up to ten strangers and say, 'Did you know I'm creative?'" My mom did not want to do that, it was really uncomfortable for her. She wanted a good grade so she had to do it. When the class came back the next time, the professor said, "Okay, now who thinks they're creative?" Everyone who did the assignment now believed they were creative.

Think about that! Just saying out loud ten times to a stranger, declaring to the universe that you are creative, had an impact in resetting their self evaluation. That was such a powerful story because as you've said, we are all children of God. We all carry embryonic Godhood in us, which means we are all creators.

I love Elder Uchtdorf's quote about whether you create families, or traditions, or gardens … there's a gazillion ways be creative. You can be creative as an engineer. You can be creative planning a garden. You can be creative in baking a wedding cake. If we want to practice becoming like our Heavenly Parents, we have to choose to create. That's one of the key attributes.

Maybe this is our challenge that we leave people with — sometime in the next week, the next month, sometime today, choose to stretch your creative muscles and find a way that you are practicing your divinity in whatever way speaks to your soul.

AC: Notice what was the first thing that came to mind. We define creativity so narrowly, as "artistic." It's not about being artistic. What's the first thing that pops into your head, and what does creativity look like in that context? That's probably your groove.

> **I think at its core, creativity is just an openness to ideas coming into your mind. That's why it feels so holy. It's a practice of opening your mind and seeing what descends, what comes into your brain. It feels the same to me as hearing God's voice.**

MK: Maybe it looks like, "I want to try …" and fill in the blank! Or, this other thing intrigues me. I like your idea of focusing on where your energy is. What would it be like to do this? The creativity part is just along the way, but you don't have to say, "I'm going to go buy some paint and an easel."

AC: I think at its core, creativity is just an openness to ideas coming into your mind. That's why it feels so holy. It's a practice of opening your mind and seeing what descends, what comes into your brain. It feels the same to me as hearing God's voice. With a lot of intention, I'm opening my heart and opening my mind, and just receiving. I'm whole, I'm here, I'm ready to act on what I receive. That is the process of creativity to me. It is spiritual work. It's exactly what prayer is to me. I'm going to sit here quietly in contemplation, to align and still my mind so I can receive. I think creativity is also that practice. Sometimes I get distracted by the word because of all the things it reminds me of, but at its essence, it is deliberate openness to receiving what comes. That is a practice that has changed me. It has helped me find and connect to God.

HIGHEST ASPIRATION

MK: That's incredible. I like the idea that creativity is bringing something into existence that didn't exist before. A friend says that her husband is wicked delighted with spreadsheets. I have never felt a thrill of divinity in opening or making a spreadsheet, but that is creative! It is creating! It is literally bringing something into existence that didn't exist before. Having this stretch, this openness to bring something forth, whatever it is, is incredibly powerful.

AC: It is holy work.

STUDY HELPS
Highest Aspiration

"Mother in Heaven" Gospel Topics essay footnote

Footnote 15: Elder Dallin H. Oaks, "Apostasy and Restoration," April 1995 general conference.

Study 1

> "Aspiration: (n) desire; ambition. Aspire: (v) be ardently desirous of something spiritual." —Webster's Handy College Dictionary (1972, p.36)

> "Aspiration: (n) a strong desire to achieve something noble; object of desire. Aspire: (v) to seek to attain or accomplish a goal." —The Merriam-Webster Dictionary (2022, p.42)

Which definitions pertain to us as we aspire to be like our Heavenly Parents?

What have you learned about being like Them? Personally, socially, and spiritually that you might not have thought of before?

If our highest aspiration is to like our Heavenly Parents, we must truly get to know Them. What can you do to get to know Them on a very personal level? What could you do in addition to your usual patterns of prayer and scripture study to stretch into new understanding?

Study 2

> We were created with the express purpose and potential of experiencing a fulness of joy. Our birthright — and the purpose of our great voyage on this earth — is to seek and experience eternal happiness. One of the ways we find this is by creating things. … The bounds of creativity extend far beyond the limits of a canvas or a sheet of paper and do not require a brush, a pen, or the keys of a piano. Creation means bringing into existence something that did not exist before — colorful gardens, harmonious homes, family memories, flowing laughter. — Elder Dieter F. Uchtdorf [1]

What are creative pursuits you did as a child? How can you bring those things back into your life?

What raw materials of creation appeal most to you in your current phase of life? What can you do to use them better?

Study 3

> The Heavenly Mother portrayed in the teachings we have examined is a pro-creator and parent, a divine Person, a co-creator, a co-framer of the plan of salvation, and involved in this life and the next. [2]

When looking at the "parts" of our divine Heavenly Mother, She is a complex being. As we strive to reach our highest aspiration, how can we become like Heavenly Mother?

How do we prepare in this life and develop these many characteristics?

What are specific goals you can set to become more like our Heavenly Parents?

Suggested Reading

"God's Love," Claire Easley, *Cherish* book 1, p.434-435
"In Your Image," Erika Larson, *Cherish* book 2, p.494-496

1. Dieter F. Uchtdorf, "Happiness, Your Heritage," October 2008 general conference.
2. Paulsen, "A Mother There," 21.

CONCLUSION

GLORIOUS

Eternal truth tells us that we've a Mother there. We have a Heavenly Mother! This truth is evidence of the fulness of the Gospel, the verity of the Book of Mormon and the Restoration of the Church on the earth for this dispensation of the fulness of times.

> **The Church is bold enough to go so far as to declare that man [and woman] has an Eternal Mother in the Heavens as well as an Eternal Father.**
> **—James E. Talmage**

This truth imparts a grand picture that gives us acuity to the divine investiture of our Savior Jesus Christ. We learn of our Heavenly Parents' nature as we learn of Him. We are aware of His nature — His love, His justice, and His mercy.

Just as Jesus Christ could not come to earth and complete His mission for us without a Mother, and as He taught us "on earth as it is in heaven" — it is the same for us. (Matthew 6:10)

We are spirit children of Heavenly Parents — a Father and a Mother. They are where we come from and They are where we are going. This knowledge is truly glorious. Knowing that we have a Mother in Heaven has the power to give us strength, increased courage, faith, and charity for others. Being aware that men were created in the image of our Heavenly Father, we can know and understand with a surety that women were also created in the image of Deity. This knowledge promotes true partnership as our heavenly model in our homes, in our wards and stakes, and as we walk through the world taking upon us the name of Christ.

Our Father and our Mother love and value us — They love us SO much that They sent Their Son. We celebrate being Their beloved children. We invite you to apply this doctrine in your life ... and feel a fulness of JOY!

James E. Talmage, "Services at the Tabernacle," Deseret News, April 29, 1902: p. 13.

CONCLUSION

I AM HERE

Jennifer Alvi

MY MOTHER'S EYES

Ashley Workman

If one day I stare Into Her eyes,

Will I be surprised to find The similarities between

Her eyes and mine?

In the mirror I see

Eyes in search of Her.

Will one day I see

Her eyes in search of me?

RESOURCES

"Mother in Heaven" gospel topics essay at churchofjesuschrist.org

HeavenlyMotherMatters.org

Instagram @HeavenlyMotherMatters

Divine Music Project

> DIVINE is the first collection of music about Heavenly Parents and our divine potential to be like Them. You can find the incredible wide-ranging music at https://www.kristinaabishoff.com/divine-project or YouTube @kristinaabishoff

In Her Image podcast

> Seeking and celebrating our Mother God through scripture, scholarship, the arts, mythology, and everyday life.

Cherish: The Joy of Our Mother in Heaven and *Cherish Volume 2: The Love of our Mother in Heaven*

> Collections of vignettes, reflections, art, poetry, and quotes from hundreds of people testifying of Heavenly Mother.

Please note that these resources cross the range of faith traditions, and, even within Latter-day Saints, they cover a range of thoughts and beliefs.

CONTRIBUTORS

Jennifer Alvi is a Certified Master Photographer and Master Artist in Idaho. She focused on Fine Art in college creating paintings, drawings, and sculpting. She collaborates to create conceptual work for clients and to enter print competitions. She and her husband raised four amazing children and are now empty nesters.

Ashli Carnicelli graduated from The Boston Conservatory with a bachelor's degree in music, vocal performance. She is a convert to the Church from her Catholic upbringing in Boston. Ashli shares her testimony on Instagram and writes a bi-monthly newsletter bearing her testimony of Christ called "The Pearls." The fulness of the gospel (especially the temple!) brings her lasting and deep joy. You can hear Ashli's singing in The Divine Music Project. She and her husband Tony are the parents of four daughters and reside in Charleston, South Carolina.

Jenna Carson is the first female chaplain for the United States military endorsed by the Church of Jesus Christ of Latter-day Saints, and currently serves in the Air Force. She is a graduate of Harvard Divinity School and is also a writer and yoga therapist. Jenna and fellow chaplain Sierra Larson began a podcast in September 2024 called "Guiding Light."

Trina Caudle is a mom of five teenagers and Scoutmaster for a Scouting America troop of girls. In her "spare time," she is a book editor for authors and small publishers, the Interview Editor for the LDS Women Project, and dabbles in crowd-sourced digitizing of historical records through the Library of Congress with her superpower of reading cursive. Trina and her family live in the Washington DC area and enjoy close access to both the Smithsonian and the Shenandoah.

Aubrey Chaves grew up near Salt Lake City, Utah. She received a degree in Elementary Education from Utah State University before teaching fourth grade for two years; she now owns a cake decorating business. Aubrey and her husband Tim are the parents of four children and live in Utah. Aubrey and Tim joined the Faith Matters executive team in 2018, and co host the Faith Matters podcast.

Tom Christofferson is the author of That We May Be One: A Gay Mormon's Perspective on Faith and Family and A Better Heart: The Impact of Christ's Pure Love, both published by Deseret Book. His career in investment management and asset servicing has allowed him to live in Europe and the US and to do business in major markets across the world. He loves to say that his Phoenix, Arizona ward is the template for a new City of Zion.

Rose Datoc Dall is a Filipina-American artist and received her BFA from Virginia Commonwealth University School of the Arts in 1990. Her figurative work is distinctive for her graphic compositions, her unconventional use of color, and her linear graphic sensibility. She is also known for her body of religious artwork and has received several awards and honors, including being in the permanent collections at the Museum of Church History and Art in Salt Lake City, Brigham Young University, and Southern Virginia University. Rose and her husband have four adult children and a growing number of grandchildren, and live in Woodland Hills, Utah.

Ginger Dall Egbert received her BFA in Illustration from Brigham Young University, and her work appears in galleries and museums across Utah. Ginger's symbolic landscapes and figures explore personal spirituality, often utilizing gold leaf and other metallic mediums to bring a feeling of transcendence and communion with the Divine.

Amber Eldredge is a painter and mother of three darling girls. She has had a paintbrush in her hand for as long as she can remember, and is inspired by the constant ups and downs of life and motherhood. She creates art to connect, to recognize the hand of God in her life, and to remind herself just how close Heaven really is.

Emily Carruth Fuller began her passion for art at an early age. Her love for creating carried her to study at Brigham Young University where she earned her BFA in Studio Arts. She achieved a life-long dream by studying abroad in Italy, followed by a two-and-a-half-year apprenticeship studying with Jeff Hein. After completing her studies, she opened her studio where she currently paints and teaches. Emily loves exploring relationship and spiritual themes in her art.

Katie Garner is constantly balancing her work as a mother of seven children with her calling as an artist. With a belief the spirit of her work carries messages directly to each viewer's heart, in a language only art can speak, Katie carefully strives to paint by the Spirit of God. She describes painting as a spiritual experience that gives her frequent opportunities to be still, appreciate the beauty of this world, and reconnect with her Heavenly Parents.

Amy Watkins Jensen is a teacher and writer with a BA in Spanish Teaching and an MA in Spanish Literature from the University of Utah. She lives in the San Francisco Bay Area, where she teaches humanities at an all-boys school for the arts. Amy is passionate about amplifying the voices of Latter-day Saints who advocate for partnership and inclusion for women in the Church. On Instagram @womenonthestand and her Substack, Women on the Stand, she highlights and shares the perspectives, stories, and insights of others alongside her own reflections. She lives with her husband Andy, their youngest daughter, and their dog, Monchi, and eagerly anticipates visits from their two older daughters, who are away at college.

McArthur Krishna With church a plane ride away from her rural India farm, McArthur started spending home church time researching and writing. Over eight years, she published 17 books, six with Deseret Book. Along the way, she has been called in to discuss women's issues in the Church with the General Women's Outreach Committee and submitted Kathy Peterson's art from the Girls Who Choose God books to be exhibited in the Conference Center. The Caitlin Connolly art from McArthur's book Our Heavenly Family, Our Earthly Family was the first art portraying Heavenly Mother published at Deseret Book and inspired the first art of Heavenly Mother to hang on Temple Square at the Church History Museum.

Julie Ann Lake-Díaz is a Chilean-American artist, raised in Salt Lake City, Utah in her childhood. Her youth through adulthood were spent in her mother's home country Chile, and later Rosario, Argentina. She received her degree in Interior Design and has studied three years in the JKR Studio Academy with J. Kirk Richards. Her figurative religious work is inspired by her family history and women in the scriptures, and she hopes to inspire others to learn from and see the divine nature of those women.

Lucy Mason, 14, is an artist, high school student, and theater kid living in Logan, Utah. She loves expressing herself through embroidery and is always learning new techniques. She has a tortoise named Quincy.

Melissa de Leon Mason is a therapist, quilter, and mom of four living in Logan, Utah. Her quilts are inspired by her experience growing up Latina on the border of Texas and Mexico. Melissa's quilts have hung at the National Quilt Museum, International Quilt Market, and QuiltCon, and have been featured in numerous publications.

Patrick Q. Mason holds the Leonard J. Arrington Chair of Mormon History and Culture at Utah State University. He has written or edited several books, including Proclaim Peace: The Restoration's Answer to an Age of Conflict and Restoration: God's Call to the 21st-Century World. He was a Fulbright Scholar in Romania in 2015 and is a past president of the Mormon History Association. Professor Mason is frequently consulted by the national and international media on stories related to Mormon culture and history. He teaches courses on Mormonism, American religious history, and religion, violence, and peacebuilding.

Janice McArthur graduated from BYU with a Bachelor and Master's degree in Education, and earned an Ed.D from Northern Arizona University in Curriculum and Instruction. Janice is a retired public school teacher and university professor now residing in Utah. She was raised in the Church with many years of committed Church service. She is a single mother of two adopted children from whom she has learned many of life's lessons. This project was a blessing and brought her much joy.

Thomas McConkie is the founder of the Lower Lights School of Wisdom and has a passion for the Wisdom teachings of the world, especially as they pertain to the Restoration. He is trained as a developmental researcher, facilitator, and mindfulness teacher, and has been in practice for over twenty years. He has written multiple books about faith transformations and created an online course at Faith Matters to integrate perspectives from the world's religious traditions as seen through the lens of the Restored Gospel.

Malinda Wagstaff Metro is an opera singer currently residing in the Pacific Northwest. She enjoys performing opera and symphonic works and teaching voice lessons. When not singing, she and her husband enjoy cooking, water-skiing, reading, writing "bad" poetry, and exploring life together.

Jody Moore is a mother of four, a Latter-day Saint, and a woman trying to figure out how to minimize resentment, overwhelm, and guilt and replace them with happiness, gratitude, and joy. She has a BA in Communications, an MA in Adult Education, and fifteen years of experience as a corporate trainer and leadership coach.

Carol Pettit is an editor who relishes words, good grammar, and connection. Asking questions is her love language. Known for her curiosity, she will pepper you with inquiry and plenty of active listening if given the opportunity. Recently accused by her 16-year-old son of being "too rapid fire," she's trying to tone it down a bit. She graduated from BYU with a degree in English and lives in Utah.

Anne Pimentel lives in Utah with her husband and four sons. She is one of the founding members of Meetinghouse Mosaic, a non-profit organization trying to diversify Christian art and educate on why representation matters. She co-authored the book Changemakers: Women Who Boldly Built Zion. She is the brains behind @the.vision.beautiful on Instagram where she boldly uses her voice to talk about Heavenly Mother, women's empowerment, and anti-racism education.

Roger Pimentel writes about the gospel and the Church, and how sometimes they even overlap. He received degrees from Brigham Young University and Arizona State University before building a career in marketing, working at Amazon and several advertising agencies. He currently lives in Utah with his wife, Anne, and their four boys. Roger writes "From the Overflow" at rogerpimentel.com and on Instagram @from.the.overflow.

Martin Pulido is the co-author of the BYU Studies article, "A Mother There: A Survey of Historical Teachings about Mother in Heaven." He also co-authored A Boy's Guide to Heavenly Mother. He believes that boys and men benefit from gaining a knowledge of and relationship with their Mother God.

J. Kirk Richards is a contemporary artist whose work engages with themes of antiquity, religion, spirituality, equality, and love. His work asks questions about modern application and implementation of religion as it relates to historical narratives and mythologies. The work often prioritizes the poetry of religious text over dogma or historical accuracy. Stylistically it often bridges or walks a tightrope between classical and abstract expression. In 2020, Kirk founded a mixed-use art space, including studio rentals, a gallery that hosts monthly themed exhibits by living professionals and semi-professionals, and a continued education art academy. Kirk lives and works at his studios in Woodland Hills, Redmond, and Provo, Utah, and in Bondsville, Massachusetts. He and his wife Amy Tolk Richards have four children.

Sarah Sabey and her husband co-wrote The Book of Mormon Storybook in an effort to bear witness to the reality of a God who loves humans, even when they do bad things, and to a world that is very good, even when it is filled with tragedy. She is working toward a PhD in 20th century literature and theology centered on the Book of Job. She and her husband also make documentaries together, and live in rural Idaho with their children.

Andy Brady Spalding is husband to Bethany and co-parent to three remarkable daughters. As a professor at the University of Richmond, he teaches and writes on anti-corruption and human rights in international sport, and expects to devote many years to the precedent-setting potential of the 2034 Salt Lake City Winter Olympics.

Bethany Brady Spalding is a co-author of the series, Girls Who Choose God and Guides to Heavenly Mother. Working for large international organizations as well as small local nonprofits, she has launched and led initiatives to empower women around the world. Bethany calls the colorful city of Richmond, Virginia home with her husband, Andy, and their three adventurous girls. She holds a masters degree from the University of London and likes bold questions, curious people, cheeky humor, and a good cup of (herbal) tea.

Kimberly Teitter is a licensed psychologist in the Salt Lake City area who works with clients of all ages to harness their inner wisdom and discover their valued life worth living. She enjoys philosophizing about human behaviors and complex systems to whomever will listen; she has contributed to podcasts, print, film, and online news. At time of writing, she is also serving as a bishop's wife and is mother to two daughters.

Melissa Tshikamba is an illustrator and figurative artist based in Utah. Her work draws inspiration from sacred imagery, the divine feminine, abstract realism, the ethereal, African symbols, mythology, cosmology, Mother Nature, and her ancestral heritage. Through her art, she explores a wide range of themes, from spirituality to identity, and seeks to challenge conventional narratives. Melissa aims to eradicate internalized racism and misogyny, enlighten and empower others, and expand the visibility of the African Diaspora's endless possibilities and perspectives. Her art serves as a reminder that everyone deserves to be seen and celebrated, and she hopes to inspire self-love in all who view her work.

Carly White is an artist attempting to paint celestial concepts with telestial hands. She has appeared in numerous shows including twice in Spiritual and Religious Art Of Utah, Springville Museum of Art and once in the Church of Jesus Christ of Latter Day Saints International Art Competition.

Alyssa Wilkinson Any time her Heavenly Parents need Alyssa to pay attention to something, They send Their message to her as a poem. Creativity in all forms — writing, photography, and even sewing elaborate Halloween costumes — has always felt sacred to her, and creativity is a passion she loves sharing with her two messy little muses. When she isn't scribbling down a thought or caring for her sweet kids, you can usually find Alyssa managing Community Outreach for her family's non-profit, Cinderella Project Utah, or going out for treats with her darling husband. Find her on Instagram @awilkinsonbooks or Facebook Alyssa Wilkinson, Author.

Ashley Workman is a creative spirit with a love for nature, animals, and poetry. Having traveled the United States, she finds peace and inspiration for her works in the great outdoors. Currently raising two delightful children in north Texas, Ashley's warm heart and dedication are felt throughout her community.

Michael Workman is a Technical Sergeant in the United States Air Force and a bomb squad instructor in Wichita Falls, Texas. He graduated from NAVSCOLEOD in 2015 to become a bomb technician and has since traveled the world supporting explosive operations and safeguarding the president, other government officials, and national dignitaries. He earned a Bachelor of Arts in Business Administration from Arizona State University and a Master of Divinity from Amridge University. Recently, he was accepted to become a Latter-day Saint Chaplain in the Air Force. He supports his wife and their two children in their growth and thriving.

www.ingramcontent.com/pod-product-compliance
Lightning Source LLC
Chambersburg PA
CBHW061747070526
44585CB00025B/2825